Sacred and Secular

Sacred and Secular
Responses to Life in a Finite World

DONALD A. CROSBY

Published by State University of New York Press, Albany

© 2022 State University of New York

All rights reserved

Printed in the United States of America

No part of this book may be used or reproduced in any manner whatsoever without written permission. No part of this book may be stored in a retrieval system or transmitted in any form or by any means including electronic, electrostatic, magnetic tape, mechanical, photocopying, recording, or otherwise without the prior permission in writing of the publisher.

For information, contact State University of New York Press, Albany, NY
www.sunypress.edu

Library of Congress Cataloging-in-Publication Data

Name: Crosby, Donald A., author.
Title: Sacred and secular : responses to life in a finite world / Donald A Crosby, author.
Description: Albany : State University of New York Press, [2022] | Includes bibliographical references and index.
Identifiers: ISBN 9781438486598 (hardcover : alk. paper) | ISBN 9781438486611 (ebook) | ISBN 9781438486604 (pbk. : alk. paper)
Further information is available at the Library of Congress.

10 9 8 7 6 5 4 3 2 1

Contents

Introduction	1
Chapter 1 Finite Earthly Time	17
Undesirability of Timeless Life	20
Illusion of Ultimate Timeless Existence	23
Hägglund's Contrast of Religious and Secular Perspectives	26
Problems with the Idea of an Everlasting Afterlife	29
Conclusion	32
Chapter 2 Fallible Human Knowledge	35
Fallibility of Human Claims to Truth	37
Unknowability of Future Beliefs	43
Dangers of Claims to Infallible Religious Beliefs	46
Inevitable and Desirable Religious Diversity	50
Conclusion	52
Chapter 3 Science, Secularity, and Religion	57
Religion's Indebtedness to the Sciences	61
Limitations of the Sciences	67
Two Conceptions of Science	69
Conclusion	78
Chapter 4 Ambiguities of Nature	81
Inanimate Nature	84
Nonhuman Animate Nature	86
The Human Side of Nature	89
Religious Affirmation of Nature	90
Conclusion	98

Chapter 5   An Urgent Common Cause   101
  A Monotheistic Response   102
  A Buddhist Response   104
  Scientific Responses   104
  Prudential Responses   109
  Moral Responses   110
  Aesthetic Responses   112
  Conclusion   114

Chapter 6   Characterizing Religion   117
  Tillich on the Narrower and Larger Concepts of Religion   120
  Schilbrack's Analysis of Definitions of Religion   122
  Religion and Ontology   126
  Conclusion   131

Chapter 7   Reconciling the Sacred with the Secular   135
  Religious and Secular Views of Reality   136
  Earlier Meanings of the Term *Secular*   137
  Concept of the Secular State   138
  Need for Religious and Secular Dialogue   142
  The Virtue of Humility   144
  Conclusion   150

Chapter 8   Western Theism and Ontological Sacredness   153
  From Radical Transcendence to Radical Immanence:
    Diana Bass's Journey of Faith   157
  The Sacredness of Nature Without God: Chet Raymo's
    Religious Naturalism   160
  Theism, Naturalism, and the Sacred   163
  Conclusion   167

Notes   171

Works Cited   173

Index   177

Introduction

Biological cells have boundaries, but the boundaries are permeable. They allow for imports from their surrounding environments but also for their own exports into it. They are thus in continual interaction with the world, taking from it but also giving to it. Boundaries are important. No cell could exist as such or function appropriately without them. In this book I suggest something similar regarding the relations of sacred and secular views of the world. They are distinct from one another and recognition and analysis of the distinction is important and necessary. But there is also a critical sense in which each contributes to the other, complementing its partiality with its own partiality, and in this way constituting a larger whole. Neither, in other words, is capable by itself of sensitizing us to the immensity of the world or the challenge and wonder of our lives as human beings in the world.

Religion contributes to the secular outlook on the world a sensibility and awareness that the secular *qua* secular lacks, namely, explicit reference and attunement to the existential and ontological import of the sacred. And secularism contributes to religion an awareness of the insistent obduracies of the world and of the contours of the prevailing culture that the sacred, in order to be in effective touch with the world and its own times, must continue to be sensitive to and to take fully into account. What results from this convergence of perspectives is a larger, more adequate awareness, but also a deeper sense of the wondrous, haunting mystery of the world—a mystery that no admixture of finite religious and secular perspectives—to say nothing of either the religious or the secular by itself—is capable of finally comprehending or dispelling.

Outright dismissal of current secular culture convicts religion of myopia and irrelevancy. And secularism, without attunement to the allure of the sacred as I shall characterize it in this book, closes itself off from a vital dimension of experience that adds much needed purpose, depth, and meaning to the world and to our lives as humans in the world. Religion and secularism, or the sacred and the secular, are thus complements to one another, not opponents of one another. Each is partial by itself. A fuller and more adequate comprehension requires what each can and should contribute to the other. Their relationship is analogous to the permeable membrane of the cell, a demarcation or border through which each contributes to the other and receives from the other essential sources of insight into the whole of life. The distinction between them remains important and is not eliminated, but the border dividing them from one another is porous, allowing for their constant interactions with one another. The metaphor of the biological cell reminds us of the necessary interrelations of the sacred and the secular.

Having said this, however, the problem is posed of how to understand the respective natures of religion and secularism in such a manner as to do justice to what I argue to be the complementary relationship between them. This is the task I undertake here. It is no easy task, to a large extent because the search for an adequate characterization of the nature of religion, understood in a comprehensive manner that takes into account the whole range of the great religions of the world, is a notoriously thorny problem. I approach the problem with trepidation, but the concept of religion I propose and develop is that religion turns finally on an attested momentous reality of the sacred—encountered, discerned, and put into practice in a wide variety of ways by the great religious traditions of the East and West and also reflected in the indigenous cultures of the world.

The secular is then to be understood as an outlook that lacks an explicit, sustained focus on the sacred as thus analyzed and understood. But this negative characterization makes room for everything else that a secular perspective can contribute to our perception and understanding, and it is necessary that we include these contributions in our concept of the secular when thinking about its relations to religion. Religion, properly understood, does not try to dictate to secular culture but rather shares with it in a spirit of learning from and relating meaningfully to its history, art, morality, politics, economics, science, and technology. And secular culture, for its part, does not try to substitute itself for religion but is sensitive to the special dimensions of or outlooks on experience, thought, and practice religion addresses and portrays.

Necessary distinctions between the secular and the religious having been made, we need to continue to do as much justice as we can to the multiple interactions and mutual contributions of the two perspectives.

We live in a dauntingly complex, demanding, mysterious world, and both religious and secular approaches to the world should be allowed to have their say. Neither approach by its limited nature can be adequate alone. Each should complement and inform the other. And it would not hurt for each to keep the other questioning and off-guard, and in that way aware of their respective limitations. There is a difference between slavishly assenting to the assumptions and maxims of either of the two perspectives, on the one hand—each perspective thereby rejecting the other out of hand—and persistently inquiring critically but appreciatively into both sets of assumptions and maxims, on the other. A disconnected, entirely self-contained cell is, after all, a dead cell, devoid of nurture and sustenance and with no way to make its distinctive contributions to a larger whole.

In the chapters of this book I expose and discuss the inadequacy of certain conceptions of the nature of religion, conceptions that turn out to be stereotypes rather than satisfactory analyses of the full range of religious outlooks as these have been developed and expressed historically, and as they continue to develop and be expressed today. Secularism is then falsely distinguished from religion on the basis of these stereotypical misunderstandings of religion.

One such stereotype is the idea that all religions or persons of religious faith by their nature are fixated on and yearn wistfully for a *timeless*, carefree state of being thought to be available to them in the future, or alternatively for a future personal existence that is believed to be *everlasting*, that is, to temporally endure forever. Some forms of religion admittedly fit this characterization, but others clearly do not. I devote this book's *first chapter* to arguments against this commonly alleged preoccupation of all types of religion and against the related notion that only secular forms of faith are capable by their nature of accepting, cherishing, and defending human existence limited to a finite time that is bounded by beginnings and endings, births and deaths. I also argue against the contention that only secular outlooks are capable of recognizing existence in time as *essential* to the meaning and value of human existence because only they sense that a life without pervasive, temporally constrained care and concern would be no life at all.

I strongly concur with the last claim about the positive value and importance of life in time but make strong objection to the allegation that affirmation and acceptance of it is somehow exclusive to the secular outlook on life and thereby excludes religion. I also argue in the first chapter that it is plainly fallacious to regard only secular outlooks and forms of life as being fervently committed to working for social justice here on earth within readily accepted conditions and limits of finite time. Religious outlooks are not generally barred by a claimed all-consuming focus on a future timeless or everlasting personal existence from exercising full responsibility to work for moral causes of the social and political type within the constraints of the temporal world. In fact, they are more often than not strongly motivated to do so. This way of drawing the distinction between the religious and the secular must also, therefore, be firmly set aside.

Chapter 2 brings under strong criticism the idea that all religions claim to have infallible or absolute knowledge about at least the most central doctrines or beliefs of their systems of thought, and that secular outlooks alone are comfortable with the idea that all the knowledge claims of humans, whether religious or otherwise, are fallible and open to critical questioning and dispute. When religious claims to infallible truths are said to be grounded in sacred texts, they show themselves to be oblivious to the ineliminable hand of human beings in the origination and writing of such texts, and to the necessary role of humans in editing, preserving, and giving canonical status to such texts. Such claims also fail to recognize that the texts would have little value, importance, or meaning apart from fallible human attempts to interpret and apply such texts to their own times, exhibiting to their fallible readers the continuing applicability of the texts to the cultures of later times.

It is simply false to think that religions *as such* can be characterized as failing to overlook the role of fallible human knowledge or claims to knowledge in the area of religion, and to contend that only secular outlooks by their very nature are willing to recognize and accept this role in all the domains of thought and experience. This stereotypical depiction of the nature of religion admittedly (and regrettably) applies to some religious outlooks and traditions of past and present times, but it does not apply to all of them. A credible distinction between religion and secularism cannot be drawn in this manner.

A central thesis of chapter 2 is that all claims to knowledge are fallible and reflect the fallibility and finitude of human beings. There is no way in which religious thought, experience, or putative revelation can immunize us against our fallibility and finitude. This fact is perhaps made especially manifest when it comes to thinking about the future. The alleged certainties of one time can become the falsehoods or at least the dubitable claims of another. This is the clear lesson of the past, and it is a lesson about scientific claims as well as about other kinds of claim to truth. There have been two major scientific revolutions so far, and we have no way of knowing whether or not there will be ones at least as major, and as overturning of fundamental, commonly accepted scientific beliefs, in the future. As creatures of time, we are caught in the contingencies and uncertainties of life in time, to return to the theme of chapter 1.

Religious claims to infallibility and absolute certitude are not only untenable. They can also be highly dangerous and disruptive to harmony, peace, and justice. The violent religious conflicts of the Thirty Years' War, following on the Protestant Reformation and the Roman Catholic Counter-Reformation, are cases in point, as are historically attested and religiously motivated pogroms, wars of colonial conquest and domination, and attempts to violently repress religious dissent. Such conflicts are not restricted to the West, although they are amply demonstrated there. They are also characteristic of the history of the East. In both parts of the world, insistence on the infallibility and absolute authority of any given set of religious beliefs, convictions, and practices can be demonic and destructive. It should be vehemently resisted and protested against in the name of religion, and not just on the basis of secular critiques of religion. And there is plenty of evidence to support the thesis that it has been and will continue to be resisted and protested by at least some genuinely religious people and deeply committed religious groups.

This last statement opens the way to the last topic of this chapter, and that is insistence on the inevitability and desirability of religious diversity. Such diversity is inevitable, given the patent diversity of cultures and historical periods throughout the world. There are indications of the commonalities of human beings throughout these cultures and periods, of course. But there are also fundamental differences. These differences are offenses to the religious mind only to the extent that the religious mind claims infallibility for its outlooks, beliefs, and practices. But viewed in another way, the differences are welcome invitations to ongoing religious enrichment, enhancement, and desirable change. Each religious person or religious tradition may turn out to have much to learn—not only from other religious outlooks, but also about both the limits and the hitherto overlooked resources of each particular outlook. Epistemic certainty is sometimes touted as the trait or goal of genuine religion, but humility is the more fundamental religious virtue. Genuine religious piety—at least as I view it—trumps claims to epistemic certainty. It does so because openness to religious truth wherever found depends on acknowledgment of the inevitable limitations of one's particular religious vision.

If it is desirable to continue to grow and develop in religious faith, given frank acknowledgment of human fallibility and finitude, then convictional religious openness is to be cherished as against the temptation to convictional religious closedness. The profound and suffusive sense of religious mystery inveighs against the temptation to think that authentic religious faith must reject, rather than welcome, religious differences. Such rejection is an in-principle denial of the cloud of mystery that necessarily surrounds, limits, and conditions all religious beliefs, forever beckoning them to further questioning, inquiry, and opening of heart and mind to other forms of religious faith.

This openness of outlook is the mark of genuine religion, as I view it, and it is a necessary antidote to prideful insistence on the infallibility of any aspect of one's own religious tradition or worldview. Religion as well as secularism can recognize and affirm the need to reject assertions of infallibility, and the religious sense of humility in the face of acknowledged surrounding mystery is a powerful safeguard against the temptation to assume or assert such claims. The fallible and the sacred are not opposed to one another. They go together and can and do work together, hand-in-hand.

Chapter 3 addresses the issue of the relations of religion to the natural and social sciences, the latter being viewed as expressions of secular perspectives on the world. Far from opposing themselves to the sciences, religions have essential and far-reaching lessons to learn from the sciences. To stand against the sciences in the name of supposed staunch religious faith is to clamp one's mind shut to what the sciences have to offer toward a more comprehensive outlook on the world. It is to reject a significant part of a culture that is deeply informed by scientific attitudes, methods, and findings, and that has been increasingly so informed since the seventeenth century CE. In other words, it is stubbornly to fly in the face of the modern world instead of seeking ways to appreciate it, learn from it, and speak with profound religious conviction and awareness to its outlooks, needs, and concerns. A religious stance that insists on disputing and flatly dismissing the contributions of the sciences shows itself to be out of touch with contemporary secular culture and its necessary place in and influence on the lives of contemporary human beings.

We can no more step out of our secular culture, replete as it is with scientifically imprinted modes of thought and practice, than we can step outside our skins. Religion has two tasks, at least, and not simply one, as far as our scientific culture is concerned. It must be in some highly important ways a critic of secular culture to the extent that secular culture fails to be responsive to the role of the sacred in human life. But it must also be sensitive to ways in which secular culture can contribute to deeper religious sensitivity and understanding, challenging it to face toward the future and not just to be mired in the conceptualities and convictions of the past. Religion does not stand still any more than do other aspects of life in the world, and the sciences are forward-looking ways of thinking and acting that religion should not feel obligated simply to fight against or ignore. The secular needs the religious, but the religious also needs the secular. There must be porous boundaries on both sides if each is to contribute meaningfully to and to derive necessary nourishment and support from the other.

An important part of this positive picture of the interrelations of religious and secular—or in this particular case, secular scientific—outlooks is recognition of the limitations of each outlook. Neither is competent to swallow the other into its own perspective. Religion that ignores contributions of a scientifically informed secular culture to its own understanding of the world and of our lives as humans in the world ignores the necessary roles of ongoing time and change in informing our conceptions of the world. Because culture is not static, neither should religion be content simply to reiterate without critical reexamination patterns of thought inherited from the distant past. Religion cannot substitute for science or do the necessary work of science, and science continues to alter our cultural perceptions of the world. These facts must be acknowledged and taken fully into account by religious thinkers. But it is also resoundingly true—at least in my considered judgment—that science cannot take the place of religion or dismiss from relevance all aspects of religion that cannot be scientifically accounted for or contained.

The final section of chapter 3 explicates two different conceptions of science. The first one concentrates on the specific contributions of the natural and social sciences to our understanding of the world and of the place of human beings in the world. Science in this interpretation points to *the various fields* of the natural sciences; it makes general reference to the plurality of these fields and to their distinctive theories and findings. The second conception of science is focused on science as a *method* of investigation rather than as a collection of scientific disciplines and the particular aid of these disciplines in adding to, or at least suggesting, different ways of understanding ourselves and the culturally informed world in which we live.

Drawing on the perceptive thought of the American philosopher John Dewey, I argue that the method of scientific thought and investigation can be profitably employed in the field of religion as well as in the fields of the natural and social sciences. Religion can be rendered as scientific in this broad methodological sense of the term *scientific*, which etymologically interpreted (Latin: *scientia*) just means *knowledge*, and by extension, *reliable knowledge*. In other words, religion so interpreted can be a source of reliable knowledge of the world, just as the natural and social sciences are commonly viewed by virtue of the extent to which they are committed to employing a method of inquiry that can bear the fruit of useful and important kinds of insight, awareness, knowledge, and understanding. I give careful attention in this chapter to Dewey's analysis of what this method of investigation should look like and to how it can and should be employed in *all* important areas of thought.

Thus, while the conclusions of religious systems of thought and those of the special sciences are different because of their different topics and concern, their respective methods of analysis can be similar. A commonality of method between secular and sacred types of inquiry brings them close to one another in approach and spirit, while their different targets of inquiry distinguish them from one another. Ongoing secular scientific thought and continuing religious inquiry are shown in this way to be complementary to one another rather than being opposed to one another, each seeking reliable knowledge in its own admittedly limited areas of thought and expertise, and each to the extent that it is willing to be committed to a common experimental method of investigation as that method is convincingly explicated by Dewey.

Chapter 4 deals with the relations of religious faith to the natural world and particularly to the ambiguities of the natural world that religion must recognize and confront. Inanimate nature has perils of many different kinds. These include natural disasters such as plagues, earthquakes, volcanic eruptions, wildfires, hurricanes, droughts, and floods. Animate, nonhuman nature adds to these inanimate threats the inevitable dangers of predation that constantly confront the lives of biological creatures. The earth-wide biological project of utilizing the energy of the sun requires that life preys on life in order to protect and preserve life. Plants, no less than animals, are caught in this tangle of predator and prey. The human side of animate nature contributes further to these ambiguities the multiple forms of cruelty, corruption, extortion, warfare, and injustice human beings have routinely inflicted on one another throughout human history and continue to inflict throughout the world today. Then there is the radical ambiguity of the threats humans pose for the whole of nonhuman nature in the form of the present ecological crisis, a crisis that endangers all species of life on earth, including the human species itself.

The evident ambiguities, uncertainties, dangers, and sufferings characteristic of the world and of life in the world are met in some religious traditions and forms of religious faith by rejection of this world and by anxious hope and anticipation of another, entirely different world to come. Such rejection might be cited as the defining trait of religion, in which case religion becomes a kind of world denial. Secularism can then be seen as world-affirmation rather than world denial, and in this way it can be distinguished from religion. While this characterization of religion certainly fits some religious outlooks and forms of faith, it does not, I contend, fit all of them. There are world-affirming as well as world-denying religions, and not all religions are fixated on an imagined perfect life to come after the grave, or on such a radical transformation of this world that it will someday be replaced by a world entirely freed of the threatening ambiguities, uncertainties, and sufferings of the present world in its inanimate, nonhuman animate, and human aspects. And not all religions seek for ways to escape from the trials of life in the world that characterize the present lives of human beings.

I discuss in this chapter three prominent world-welcoming and world-affirming types of religion, and I seek to show in addition that the idea of a world entirely free of ambiguities is not even a conceivable world. It is not conceivable partly because a world of orderly, predictable laws is a necessarily ambiguous world, while a world devoid of laws that can sometimes hurt instead of help sentient creatures, is no world at all but a hopeless chaos. And even if such a world were conceivable, it would necessarily eliminate the possibility of human freedom, for reasons I adduce and discuss. Human freedom is ambiguous because it can be a source of evils, and sometimes demonic evils, as human history forcefully demonstrates. But human freedom lies at the heart of what it means or can mean to be a responsible person. It is thus a highly desirable capability, despite the acknowledged ambiguities to which it can and does inevitably give rise.

I bolster my defense of this-worldly religion with discussion of three prominent examples of it in the continuing history of various types of religious faith. The first is a defense of *pantheism* mounted by the German Protestant theologian of the nineteenth century Friedrich Schleiermacher; the second is *Daoism*; and the third is the versions of *religious naturalism* that have come to the fore—especially in the United States—in recent years. These three outlooks are both deeply religious and firmly world-affirming. Their affirmation of this world, with all of its ambiguous realities and possibilities, does not demarcate them as secular, meaning that basing the distinction between religion and secularism on world-denial and world-acceptance respectively, does not meet the test of either critical or historical analysis. Nature as it is can be welcomed, affirmed, celebrated, and loved in the name of religion and fully acknowledged as inherently sacred.

Moreover, such world-affirming religious outlooks can interact with positive secular perspectives on the world in mutually supportive manners. They can do so in ways that world-denying religious perspectives make much more difficult, even to the point of rejecting everything that does not fit into their other-worldly perspectives. Anxious preoccupation with a supposed perfect, non-ambiguous world to come, or intensive search for a present route of escape from the challenges and tribulations of an engaged earthly life, makes world-denying religions unsuitable for extensive interactions with secular cultures and secular worldviews.

In *Chapter 5* I direct attention to the earth-wide ecological crisis of the present century. I discuss here some ways in which religious-minded and secular-minded people and religious and secular institutions can explore and implement ways of responding to the crisis and working together to alleviate its destructive effects. I cite examples of a Protestant Christian leader, an engaged Buddhist center, and a scientist who lays heavy stress on the sacredness of nature's creative processes, exhibiting in these ways how both religious and secular outlooks and resources can be drawn upon in order to elicit awareness of imminent ecological disaster and to motivate urgent resolve to fight against it. With the example of the biologist Stuart Kauffman, I show how both secular scientific and religious convictions can join forces in this fight.

The battle can also be joined for a combination of scientific and moral reasons, as I demonstrate in the case of the biologist E. O. Wilson. I also briefly describe what philosopher Kurt Baier calls *the moral point of view* and call for its extension to nonhuman animals as well as human ones. There are also powerful prudential and aesthetic motivations for acknowledging and seeking ways to counter the threat of environmental disaster in our time. Different reasons and motivations can thus combine, each leading to the similar conclusion of faithful respect for earthly nature's well-being and the resolve to work with passionate conviction for its restoration, repair, and continuing creativity. I emphasize the magnitude and the urgency of structural and institutional transformations—and not just those of individual consciousness and commitment—that lie before us in the face of threatening ecological disaster.

Religion has a definite role to play in this regard, and it can and must join hands with secular outlooks and pursuits to protect and preserve the ecological home we humans share with all other living creatures. But in order to play this necessary role, religion must be confessedly world-affirming and not morbidly world-ignoring, world-impugning, or world-denying. That it has the proven, effective ability and promise to be the former rather than the latter, and to cooperate fully with the secular aspects and resources of culture for the sake of doing so, is the demonstrable thesis of the fifth chapter

Chapter 6 is devoted to the task of providing an adequate depiction of the distinctive nature of religious faith and of showing in this manner how religion differs from secularism. It also seeks to show how religion and secularism, despite their palpable differences, can draw on their many commonalities of function, belief, and commitment to work together for the integrity and well-being of human society, of all forms of life on earth in their respective ecological niches, and of the inanimate features of the whole earth as well. The chapter acknowledges the many similarities of function that are shared by religious and secular perspectives, but it also highlights the ontological focus and commitment that I argue to be the distinguishing characteristic of religion in its various forms. In concentrating on religion's central ontological commitment, I follow the lead of American philosopher Kevin Schilbrack. But I differ from his interpretation of how this distinctive ontological focus should be described.

What is distinctive about religion as I view it is its preoccupation with the ontological status or role in reality of the *sacred* as religiously conceived and revered. The chapter presents a list of defining traits of the sacred and provides examples of how these traits are exemplified in some of the great world religions and in an indigenous religious culture of North America. In all such cases, the sacred is believed to have a central, dominant, pervasive ontological status and not just to be an imagined ideal. Secular outlooks, in contrast, are not marked by this distinctive ontological focus, either professedly or implicitly. The latter may have ontological commitments that differ from the sacred as I describe it. These commitments can be explicit or implicit.

In spite of this critical difference between religious and secular forms of faith, there are many areas of overlap between them that permit of shared projects, endeavors, and concerns of many kinds. The two are not so much opposed to one another in all areas of thought and practice as different from one another in one crucial respect. Religion turns on an explicit ontology of the sacred, while secular outlooks do not. But this difference permits many overlaps of mutual appreciation, awareness, and conviction. These overlaps should be exploited and implemented to the maximum degree rather than being ignored or minimized by either side.

This statement anticipates the topic and concern of *chapter 7*, which is the pressing need for reconciliation of sacred and secular views of the world. In this chapter I explore some earlier meanings of the term *secular*, noting how the term came eventually to stand outside of, rather than being included within, the specific orbit of religion. I discuss the concept of the secular state, showing how it has mainly been designed to be neutral with regard to distinctively religious traditions, institutions, practices, and beliefs, thus allowing each of them to flourish unimpeded by the state. The seventeenth-century philosopher John Locke's argument is brought into play in this regard. Locke observed that honest religious piety cannot be commanded or enforced by the state because a person can only be freely invited and persuaded to have sincere religious convictions of any kind.

To think otherwise, as states with a particular established religious institution could be construed to think and are so construed by Locke, especially in light of the religious violence of the Thirty Years' War and of other disruptive and destructive religious conflicts of recent memory in his own time, is to make these states encouragers and supporters of personal hypocrisy, dishonesty, and insincerity when it comes to religious convictions. It is also to give states with an established religion incentive and sanction for wars against states with different established religions. A religiously neutral or secular state should therefore be seen as a champion of religious freedom and of genuine, freely chosen religious faith, and not as being opposed to religion.

This is one of the principal ways in which secularism and religion can be seen as cooperating with and assisting one another—in keeping with the main theme of this chapter. I contrast this approving view of religious neutrality on the part of states with the claim by ultra-conservative religious thinkers in the United States today who claim that the country has always constituted itself as a Christian state and that it should continue to strive to act and be regarded as such. This view not only founders on historical grounds; it is opposed to a central motto of the United States, namely, *E pluribus unum* (out of many, one). The "many" in this case is the plurality of religious outlooks and traditions brought to its shores that are allowed free rein to be cherished and practiced in the United States. The "one" is the consensus about fundamental political and policy principles of nationhood that can be drawn upon by religious as well as secular persons where neither is allowed to usurp or dominate the other.

In the pursuit of further clarification of the nature of religion, a clarification that is needed if we are properly to perceive the differences between religious and secular outlooks, I take issue in this chapter with the idea that religious faith can be accurately described as the state of being ultimately concerned with whatever is believed to be ontologically ultimate. This conception of the nature of religious faith was endorsed by the German-American theologian Paul Tillich. I note that secular people may also have versions of faith that turn on assumed ontological ultimates, and I describe some of these other kinds of ultimate commitment. Thus, it is not mere ultimacy that characterizes the object of distinctively religious faith. Instead, it is the ontological *ultimacy of the sacred* that accurately defines the object of religious faith, the sacred being understood as I describe it in chapter 6.

Proponents of religious and secular kinds of faith are not thereby cut off from meaningful and fruitful dialogue. They can have much to learn from one another's different perspective on the world. But they can only do so with attitudes of openness, receptivity, and humility on both sides. Their differences are not to be discounted in such ongoing encounters and conversations. Were there no significant differences, there would be little to learn from their dialogues. Attempts to downplay or ignore all of the differences would mean an attitude of condescension on either side, a failure to take seriously the strength of conviction on the two sides. Honest and effective ongoing dialogue between those holding religious and secular views, or among disputants of strictly religious persuasions, or among those of strictly secular persuasion, does not require an outlook of epistemological relativism. Instead, it requires an outlook of convictional openness, where convictions as well as receptivity to opposing points of view are respected and given their due. All such disputants, after all, live in a common world and must find ways to cooperate with and learn from one another in the world.

I therefore strongly encourage in this chapter the need for persistent, ongoing interaction and dialogue among religious and secular people and their respective commitments and traditions of thought. Their intersections of agreement can be a basis for their explorations of areas of disagreement in a spirit of honest, open-minded investigation. Having the disagreements brought out into the open can have two important effects. It can make the participants in dialogue more fully conscious of the nature of their disagreements, and it can also invite shared investigations into assumptions and reasons underlying the disagreements. Effective critical thought can thus be encouraged on both sides, with a possible widening and deepening of each perspective.

It is one thing to have assumptions about which we may not be fully aware. It is another to bring them to the surface and subject them to shared critical analysis. Such an approach can lessen the disparities between religious and secular outlooks and broaden their areas of possible agreement and common effort. Honesty and humility are required on both sides of such dialogues if they are to have their desired effects. The point applies to religious participants in such dialogues as much as it does to secular ones when the two are brought into conversation. Blind, unthinking, adamant opposition of the one to the other, and the attempt to impose the one on the other, miss the chance of much to be gained from their mutual sharing and willing cooperation. Neither side is capable of having all of the truth needed for dealing with life in a perilous world, and neither side is in possession of some infallible, unrevisable basis for the truths it claims. The sacred and the secular are complementary to one another in numerous ways rather than being necessarily opposed to one another.

Opposition to this irenic view comes markedly from two opposed sides at present, that of the vehement, anti-religious, scientistic secularism of thinkers like Richard Dawkins and influenced and represented by the logical positivism of the early twentieth century, on the one side, and that of the ultraconservative Christians who insist on the infallibility of their Bible in all areas of thought and practice, on the other. I mention the latter but do not go into detail in discussing it. But I devote some concerted attention to the former, showing how both Dawkins and the positivists exhibit an attitude of close-minded intolerance when it comes to all things religious.

I criticize these kinds of stark opposition between religion and secularity, seeing them as narrow, uninformed, lacking interest in being better informed, and destructive of the need for both sides to be brought into useful and necessary relationship with the other. Each has perspectives, values, and commitments from which the other has much to learn and gain. Each deserves full recognition, respect, and acceptance in a just, peaceful, well-ordered society. In order for this crucial open-spirited and open-minded posture to be cultivated and maintained, it is important that we continue to reflect on and aspire to do justice to the respective natures and roles of religion and secularism, to their significant differences as well as their important areas of overlap and common concern. This is the major thesis I defend in this book.

Chapter 8 is devoted to discussion of the relations between a particular kind of theistic view and a religious naturalist view of the world, and of the place of humans in the world. The theistic view is that of Christian author Diana Butler Bass, and the naturalistic one is that of professor of physics Chet Raymo. These two writers are tantalizingly close to one another's basic religious commitments, despite the fact that Bass gives a prominent place to God in the articulation of her outlook, while Raymo does not. However, the focus of both of them is intensively on the here-and-now natural world rather than on some kind of supernatural realm. It is also the case that each, in her or his distinctive fashion, exhibits a profound level of respect for and a ready openness to interaction with secular worldviews.

Bass locates God squarely in the natural world rather than in some kind of supernatural heaven, and Raymo draws primarily on the secular discipline of physics and other natural sciences in maintaining the same focus on the natural world. Bass's concept of God's *character*, in contrast with her passionate insistence on God's *location* in the world, is left vague—so much so in fact as to bring her theology extremely close to Raymo's religious naturalism. In consequence, both of their views, while explicitly and emphatically religious in their insistence on the presence of the ontological sacred throughout nature, are also warnings against restricting the scope and character of religious faith in general to its more familiar historical forms.

Religion need be no more fixed or unalterable in its fundamental modes of development and expression than is secular culture. Both can face toward the future and not just be frozen in the past. Each can fruitfully influence the other in the present, as can easily be shown always to have been true, whether explicitly or implicitly, in the past. Religion and secularism are aspects of the same cultural system at any given time, and each aspect needs to be given its due. To set them sharply and permanently against one another is to be guilty of regrettable close-mindedness and opacity of outlook. They are demonstrably not the same, but they should also not be set in complete opposition to one another. The two authors focused on in this final chapter make this lesson apparent in eloquent and persuasive detail.

I appreciate the work of two unidentified readers from State University of New York Press who took the time to read a draft of this book and to make helpful critical comments concerning it. I am also grateful to SUNY Press editor James Peltz, who has patiently and with utmost courtesy guided me through the process of presenting my book proposal for consideration by the press during the difficult time of the COVID-19 pandemic. Production editor Diane Ganeles was prompt, considerate, and helpful throughout development of the book's text. And as always, I want to express my special gratitude to my wife Pam, who has read through this book with me, as with most of my others, with a careful eye for detail and encouraged me to rethink aspects of it that needed clarification and improvement. The final outcome, of course, is my own, and I accept responsibility for it, for good or ill.

Chapter One

Finite Earthly Time

> We can . . . describe religious and secular faith as two different motivational structures. If I am motivated by *religious* faith, the goal of my striving is to rest in peace. I may never achieve such peace, but *if* my desire were fulfilled I would be free from all care. My ultimate concern is to have no concern.
>
> In contrast, if I am motivated by *secular* faith, being concerned is part of what I strive for. Even if my desires were absolutely fulfilled—even if I lived in the midst of an achieved social justice, blissfully happy with my beloved, and with my work flourishing—I would still be concerned, since everything I care for must be sustained over time and will be lost. Moreover, the risk of loss is why I care, why it matters to me what happens, and why I am compelled to remain faithful.
>
> —Martin Hägglund (2019: 77)

I argued in a previous book (2011) that there are two major types of faith, namely, religious and secular faith. I developed there a theory of the nature of faith, showing how faith thus described can have religious and secular forms. It is wrong, therefore, to identify faith or communities of faith solely with religious outlooks and commitments. The present book is dedicated to further analysis of the two kinds of faith and of their relationships. Such analysis is required because the natures of the two and their interrelations are often, in my view, mischaracterized and misconceived. Overlaps of the two, I shall argue, are important and revealing, not just the differences between them. The two kinds of faith can have shared beliefs, values, and commitments despite their differences. But the essential differences also need to be made as clear as possible.

I shall in due course in this book explicate and defend a religious view of the world that owes much to present-day secular culture in its many manifestations and that is in many ways deeply indebted to the natural sciences while not being uncritically bound to or reducible to them. In doing so, I shall show why a view of the world that may be judged in many of its respects as exclusively secular can in fact be avowedly and distinctively religious. The pivot point of this claim, and of the arguments on its behalf, is the crucial concept of the sacred. The term *sacred* is employed in various ways in secular discourse, as I shall readily acknowledge, but I also argue for its profound specifically religious meanings and for the central place of these meanings in religious visions of the world.

The focus of this chapter is on the relations of secular and religious faiths to the finitude, risks, and uncertainties of our lives in *time*—lives that begin with the dates of our births and end in the dates of our deaths. In the epigraph to this chapter, Swedish scholar Martin Hägglund, professor of comparative literature at Yale University, draws the distinction between secular and religious forms of faith entirely on the basis of their different ways of responding to time.

Secular faith, he argues, affirms the finitude of time, with all of its threats and dangers, and with its ultimate end in death, because only in the face of such finitude is there reason to care about anything or anyone. All kinds of *religious* faith, in contrast, at least by his reckoning, have as their ultimate goal escape from temporal existence and release from the often anxiously demanding and fretful care that is the necessary accompaniment of life in time. For secular faith, a life without care would be pointless and absurd, while for religious faith, an individual life without care is the ultimate goal. According to Hägglund, a life without care, a life of total immunization against the conditions, threats, responsibilities, and concerns of finite temporal existence, would be *no life at all*. Without awareness of impending death, life would lose its sense of urgency and responsibility. With the prospect of a future of endless tomorrows, we would be lulled into complacency and seduced into putting off indefinitely the performance of difficult choices and actions (2019: 12–13).

Thus secular faith resolutely affirms the finitude of time and of life in time, while religious faith passionately hopes for blissful release from the ravages and cares of time. This is Hägglund's way of drawing the fundamental distinction between what it means to live with secular faith as opposed to a life guided by religious faith. He is no friend to religious faith understood in this manner. He is convinced that no thoughtful person should be either. Finite life in finite time, life that stretches between the alpha and omega of birth and death and is subject to the challenges, gifts, burdens, and vicissitudes of time should be welcomed rather than deplored.

For Hägglund, this is the gist of the secular outlook and creed—a creed that courageously accepts and affirms the opportunities and constraints, the joys and sorrows, the gains and losses, of temporal existence. A life freed from the burdens of time is for him no life at all. It is therefore futile to strive or hope for such a "life," here on earth, as in the quest for nirvana (51–52), or beyond the grave. Life without care, immortal existence without risk, need, or concern, is for Hägglund anything but a desirable goal. The idea of it is a contradiction, an implicit rejection of life itself. Religious people may unthinkingly yearn for it, but secular people see it for what it is, a will-o'-the-wisp without form or substance.

As he puts the matter in this chapter's epigraph, "the risk of loss is why I care, why it matters to me what happens, and why I am compelled to remain faithful." Without the risk of loss, without the fervent hope of desirable things being "sustained over time" in the face of the uncertainties of life in time, there would be no point or purpose in caring. Everything would then be timelessly or everlastingly what it is with no prospect of death or deleterious change, meaning that there would be no need or use for my efforts or strivings or for those of anyone else. There is nothing to be concerned about, nothing that requires timely attention or care. My decisions and actions are in this way superfluous.

This scenario is for Hägglund the direct opposite of a meaningful life and, indeed, of life as such. Those who aspire toward timeless eternity, absence of care, and final rest as the ultimate goal of life on earth—and for him, this group encompasses *all persons of religious rather than secular persuasion*—suffer from a grave delusion. They yearn for a personal existence beyond their deaths that is freed at last from the yoke of time. But they fail to notice that timeless or endless "life"—when properly analyzed—is not only the negation of all possibility of leading a purposeful life; it is also indistinguishable from total annihilation or death.

I am in full agreement with Hägglund's argument in two respects, but I firmly disagree with him in another. I agree that yearning for timeless or endless existence is misguided and futile, and that such existence is a contradictory idea. I shall indicate my own reasons for thinking these two assertions to be true. But I strongly disagree with his notion that it is in the very nature of having a religious outlook on life and the world to aspire ultimately toward a timeless afterlife or some other kind of deliverance from temporal existence. I grant that many religious people and traditions do give prominent voice to such an aspiration, but I reject Hägglund's claim that all religious persons and traditions do so or must do so in virtue of their being religious. To draw the distinction between secular and the religious kinds of faith on this basis is a mistake that suffers from too narrow an understanding of religion and too simplistic a conception of the relations between secular and religious stances.

I want to examine further and defend Hägglund's commendable idea that not only is timeless life wholly undesirable, but that there is no possibility of there being any such thing. It is therefore futile to yearn for and aspire toward an imagined timeless life. I shall defend this case on these two fronts. First, such existence is not even desirable, not something to be intelligently sought for as the chief aim of life. Second, even if it were desirable, it is not really possible or conceivable.

Then, third, I shall take issue, among other things, with Hägglund's contention that it is in the nature of all types of religious faith that they zealously seek for some kind of ultimate release from finite time, a risk-free, carefree mode of existence, whereas secular faith by its nature accepts and affirms the cares and concerns of finite temporal life. This way of distinguishing secular from religious faith—the central concern of the present book—must be rejected, and for compelling reasons.

Finally, I shall argue in a fourth section that belief in *everlasting* life or life without impending death—as distinguished from *timeless* life—is also untenable. But, again, I do not think that commitment either to timeless or everlasting existence marks a decisive dividing line between religious and secular forms of faith.

Undesirability of Timeless Life

We sometimes, and especially in times of great sorrow or stress, dream of becoming immune to the demands of life in time—of entering into some kind of completely restful, peaceful, undisturbed, and forever imperturbable state. But as Hägglund warns us, to wish for such a state is the height of folly. I want here to develop reasons supplemental to his for drawing this conclusion. There is no past or future in an eternal or timeless state. We could not reflect on the past and draw lessons from it concerning our actions in the present. There would be no malleable present with which to respond to the influences of the past. There would be no future for us to look forward to and plan for, and no undesirable aspects of an envisioned future for us to seek to avoid.

With no future, there would be no role for hope. In his best-selling and frequently reprinted book *Man's Search for Meaning*, psychiatrist Viktor Frankl emphasizes the prominence of the possibility of hope for the grievously suffering and inhumanely treated inmates of the concentration camps of Hitler's Germany—among whom he was one—and for human beings in general:

> Any attempt at fighting the camp's psychopathological influence on the prisoner by psychotherapeutic or psychohygienic methods had to aim at giving him inner strength by pointing out to him a future goal to which he could look forward. Instinctively, some of the prisoners attempted to find one on their own. It is a peculiarity of man that he can only live by looking to the future. . . . And this is his salvation in the most difficult moments of his existence, although he sometimes has to force his mind to the task. (2006: 72–73)

A so-called timeless life offers no prospect of hope or of the striving toward the possibilities of an envisioned future that is essential to sane and healthy human life.

Also, with no future there would be no possibility of future-oriented, genuinely free decisions and actions. Not only would free acts be impossible in the absence of an open future, but there would be no way for us to make any difference by means of such actions. Freedom requires a future amenable to change, and a timeless realm is a fixed realm, impervious to change. We can hope to contribute to the betterment of the world only if aspects of it still need improvement, and only if we are free. But if it is already timelessly perfect, then our actions can make no difference. So decisions of any kind would not only be unintelligible but ineffectual even if they were somehow possible, that is, they would be unable to bring about any kind of change in a changeless world. In other words, we humans could have no autonomy, responsibility, use, or beckoning goals in a timeless state of being. Not only would our putative acts have no consequences, but they would no longer be available to us because acting takes time. Thus, there could be no such thing as purposive striving or ongoing development of our personal characters and contributions. We would be frozen solid in an unchanging and changeless present.

At another place in his book, Frankl observes that "mental health is based on a certain degree of tension between what one has already achieved and what one still ought to accomplish, or the gap between what one is and what one should become. Such a tension is inherent in the human being and therefore is indispensable to mental well-being." This tension is nothing other than the human being's "will to meaning" (as Frankl terms it), and he cannot conceive of a healthy human life without either its latent or its developing presence (104–5). In a timeless world, such searching and striving toward the future for personal realization of existential meaning and value could not exist.

We would, in effect, lose our individuality and integrity in a timeless state of being. We could no longer be the unique, particular persons we were on earth. It would therefore not be we humans plaintively imagined to survive and thrive in a timeless state but—if at all—some phantasmagoric shade of our past existence. To strive for such a timelessness and absence of care and concern in the future would be foolishly to wish to trade challenging, meaningful *adventure* for bland, supine *safety*, the safety of nonentity, inaction, and lack of hope for anything different from what already is and must unchangeably and everlastingly be. Such a static state, even if possible, would be one of unbearable tedium, a condition stripped of any desirable reason for continuing to exist. It would thus be pointless and absurd. To long for ultimate escape from time is to mistakenly long for the annihilation of the integrity and meaning of our earthly personhood, not, as we might imagine, for a fullness and completion of our true being.

Thus Hägglund is entirely right to dismiss such yearning as a desirable goal and to be deeply critical of religious outlooks that hold up such a goal as humanity's ultimate aspiration and destiny. I agree with him entirely in this respect and have mounted a similar critique of one prevalent religious conception of an imagined perfect world and blissful afterlife in my book *Living with Ambiguity* (2008: 25–32). A supposed timeless heaven or nontemporal state of being is in fact an ominous vision of hell, a forfeiting of all that can give point and significance to human life. It is implicitly a rejection of life itself.

The conception of it, when subjected to unblinking analysis, turns out to be a kind of gross, pervasive, thoughtless *nihilism*—hardly something to be ardently sought for and desired. But I shall contend in the third section of this chapter that this conception does not constitute the dividing line between religious and secular visions of life—as Hägglund believes—because it is not true that *all* religious outlooks are necessarily committed to it as the ultimate aim of human life. I shall argue that it is *not* in the very nature of religion as such to do so. Some religious stances closely match his portrayal, to be sure, and he shows this to be the case by extensive and intriguing analysis of the thought of notable religious thinkers such as Saint Augustine and Søren Kierkegaard. He cites the Buddhist goal of nirvana as another case in point. But not all religions or religious persons yearn for some sort of ultimate timeless state or must do so in order to be truly and fully religious. Hägglund confuses a part with a whole of which it is only a part.

He thinks that religious faith, in order to address the real requirements and needs of life in the temporal world, and in order to expose and fight effectively against the many bastions of social injustice," must be *converted into secular faith* and be devoted to social justice as an end in itself" (2019: 332; my italics). This statement exposes a far too narrow understanding of the history of religions—erroneously seeing all religions and all versions of particular religious traditions as revolving around the goal of ultimate timeless existence as the sole end in itself—and a far too broad understanding of what it means to have a secular kind of faith, as if *only secular faith* fervently concerns itself with social justice as an inherently important end. I shall defend this analysis in the third section of this chapter, but now I want to show that the goal of ultimate timeless existence is not only a thoroughly undesirable but also an impossible and thus a delusionary goal.

Illusion of Ultimate Timeless Existence

I argued at length in a recently published book (2020) that time is *primordial*, meaning that it is not reducible to something more fundamental than itself, it cannot have an absolute beginning or ending, nor can there be some realm of existence of any kind that is outside of time or immune to the effects of time. I argued further that varying rates of change in different inertial frames are not identical with what underlies those changes and is presupposed by them, namely, time itself. Hence, what is measured by differing rates of change is not reducible to them. Moreover, the history of the universe and of the earth is commonly marked by specific dates, and these tacitly acknowledge a nonrelative temporal sequence of events applicable to the universe as a whole. There are agreed-on probable dates among scientists for the Big Bang, for example, another for the beginning of cosmic inflation, one for the beginning of the formation of stars, one for the origin of the solar system, and one for the beginning of life on earth. A universal passage of time is in this way thought to be essential to an emergent and ever-emerging universe such as ours demonstrably is.

By all the available evidence, existent being as such is becoming and changing. There is no such thing as static existence anywhere or anywhen. I contend in the 2020 book that arguments for the denial of the ultimate reality of time set forth by many contemporary physicists fail to be plausible for telling reasons, including those of inconsistency with the qualitative, time-saturated character of everyday firsthand human experience, due recognition of the mistake of interpreting time as a creature of change instead of correctly seeing change as presupposing time, and the coming into being and passing out of being of everything that we encounter on every hand and that affects all existing creatures and things without exception. The "without exception" includes the physicists themselves, who in the fullness of time are born, mature, grow old, and die, as well as philosophers and others who presume to deny the ultimate reality of time. The blend of varying degrees of continuity and novelty essential to the nature of time is essential to all that exists in time, and this means everything that can properly be said to exist.

Restless volatility and ceaseless process mark the quantum realm as it is currently portrayed and whose mysteries are at least partially understood by today's physicists, and it ultimately characterizes everything on earth as well as everything in the farthest regions of intergalactic space, as each of these regions is currently described by such sciences as those of physics, chemistry, biology, ecology, and cosmology (or astrophysics). Everywhere there is volatility; nowhere is there such a thing as complete stasis or rest.

Every human life is experienced as changing as it unfolds over the years. We cannot live in the past or stay in the present. We may nostalgically try to go backward and undo or relive the past, but this is clearly impossible. And we cannot reasonably expect the present to stay forever the same. We are born at some particular time and must die at some other particular time. All of our aspirations, regrets, achievements, and strivings—whether as particular individuals or as whole societies and civilizations—involve constraints, opportunities, challenges, possibilities, beginnings and endings posed by the inexorable passage of time. As new factual situations emerge, they give expression to new real possibilities, possibilities that were not there earlier but that have also emerged over the course of time.

"Timeless life," whether of humans or of any biological organism, is a contradiction. There would be no lives on earth of any kind were it not for processes of biological evolution occurring over billions of years, and the complex systems of material organization that underlie and make life possible also had to undergo intricate processes of change over massive stretches of time. Matter itself as we currently experience and understand it is the outcome of processes of energetic transformation beginning with the Big Bang origin of the present universe, some 13.8 billion years ago. Atoms and molecules, as well as the four fundamental physical forces and subatomic particles on which they depend, are the consequences of process, as are the macroscopic entities of multifarious kinds they make possible.

The universe continues to be processive in its ultimate nature. And process and change, as I indicated earlier, presuppose primordial time. Furthermore, there would be no such thing as life apart from gestation, growth, maturation, reproduction, and decline—all temporal factors. Finally, and as we have already seen, a so-called human life outside of time would not only be pointless and meaningless, it would cease to be anything meaningfully described as life.

Nontemporal existence, by every cogent and relevant empirical and theoretical indication, is unimaginable and unrealizable. To posit it as the goal of life is like positing a circle as the goal of a straight line. So long as the line remains straight, it cannot be circular. So long as there is life, human or otherwise, it cannot be nontemporal. The temporal cannot originate from the completely nontemporal or culminate in the completely nontemporal. Even the terms *originate* and *culminate* are temporal terms that must, in this context, assume what they intend to deny.

So long as human and nonhuman life and everything else in nature as we know them are temporal and changing, they cannot by some twitch of a magical wand—or by some feat of even the most sophisticated, complex, reasoning, whether scientific, religious, philosophical, or otherwise—be convincingly shown to be even potentially nontemporal and unchanging. They cannot in our own case as humans without positing an unbridgeable dualism between their temporal present life and a supposed timeless life to come, or between this present life and a timeless mode of existence allegedly available to us in the depths of the here and now—two incoherent dualisms without any conceivable points of overlap, intersection, or relationship between their diametrically opposed realms. "Timeless reality" may sound like a meaningful phrase, but it applies only to fanciful, abstract conceptions of reality, not rightly to those of concrete existence.

The goal of timeless existence or perpetual rest is a goal without substance or meaning, and it is, as Hägglund correctly reasons, foolish to posit it and aspire toward it as the ultimate aim of human life. Work and rest are correlatives. Neither is possible apart from the other. Endless work is physically impossible, to say nothing of being desirable. The same is true of endless rest. Without work as its correlative, there would be nothing from which to rest. And without striving in and through obstacles and opportunities posed by time, human life would not only cease to have sustaining zest and meaning. It would no longer be intelligible as life.

Hägglund's Contrast of Religious and Secular Perspectives

Hägglund's reasoning ceases to be convincing, however, when he argues that it is in the very nature of all religious outlooks on the world that they posit some kind of escape from the strictures of time as the ultimate goal of human life, and when he goes on to argue that the observation marks the demarcation between the secular—which readily accepts and affirms the reality of time—and the religious, which according to him does not.

A notable exception to his thesis is the fervently engaged life of the Jewish people of the period of the development of the principal part of the Hebrew Bible that stretches from about the tenth century BCE to the sixth century BCE. Here the focus is squarely on this earthly life, not on some imagined heavenly life to come. In fact, there is no indication of the existence of such a future life. And the focus is one of intense preoccupation with issues of social justice, as is shown by the writings of such biblical prophets as Jeremiah, Isaiah, Amos, and Micah. The antidote to social and individual evils does not lie in some sort of future existence but in the present collective life of Israel as a people bound to God by a sacred covenant.

And God—far from existing in and restricted to some imagined timeless realm—is a God who is intimately involved in, and whose nature is continuously being revealed within, the historical experiences of the Jewish people. God's overarching concern is for social justice, for exemplary just actions of the nation as a whole and for just treatment of all peoples, including the strangers, the poor, and the weak. This religious God is also an intensely moral and political God.

The prophet Amos, for example, warns that God desires not just solemn priestly ceremonies, songs, and sacrifices but justice rolling throughout the nation Israel "like an ever-flowing stream" (Amos 5:21–24). And the prophet Micah states that God is interested above all else in humans learning to practice justice and mercy toward one another, and in their being humbly dedicated to the will and purpose of their just and righteous Creator who is intimately involved in their temporal lives (Micah 6:6–8). Specific divine indictments of current social injustices suffuse these two texts, as they do the prophetic literature of the Hebrew Bible in general. The focus of Amos and Micah, as that of all of the prophets of the classical biblical period that culminates in the sixth century after the Jewish exile in Babylon, is on *this life*, not on a supposed life beyond the grave. Here-and-now social justice is their passionate concern. Contrary to Hägglund's thesis, preoccupation with social justice is not the sole preserve of secular-minded traditions or peoples. It is the fundamental theme of Jewish religiosity throughout the classical biblical period.

Moreover, as Philip Jenkins, professor of history at the Institute for Studies of Religion at Baylor University, reminds us,

> In the canonical Hebrew Bible, concepts of the afterlife are pallid and indistinct. In the pre-Exilic Jewish world, individuals who died survived at best as shades who had little distinct identity. . . . The Bible refers often to Sheol, the place of the dead, but this miserable place was not reserved for notorious sinners or wrongdoers. Regardless of one's virtue or piety, the ultimate fate of humanity was the grave, with its maggots and worms. (2017: 13)

Neither a timeless nor an everlasting afterlife, then, is the ultimate aim of the intensely religious Jewish people in the biblical period. The latter became the concern of some but not all of Jewish theologians and rabbis later. Even in the New Testament period of the first century CE, the Sadducees continued to reject belief in life beyond the grave, while the Pharisees affirmed it. Genuine religion without focus on an endless life beyond the grave is clearly both historically manifest and readily conceivable.

And not all religious conceptions of an afterlife are necessarily conceptions of a timeless realm devoid of ongoing historical passage, striving, or change. When Jews in later times speak of an afterlife, they typically do not see it as timeless rest, devoid of change. Twentieth-century rabbi, prolific author, and revered exponent of Judaism Isidore Epstein writes that, for Judaism, immortality means continuing to be a "co-worker with God." It is not "merely a survival beyond the grave, but the homecoming of the spirit or the soul of man to the further cultivation and development of the divine relationship made manifest on this state of life" (1964: 141).

Life and work go on in the afterlife. It is not just a timeless state of being with no challenging expectations or demands placed on the human spirit.

It is certainly not the case for Jewish religion that working for justice must be regarded as a solely secular and not in any way truly religious kind of endeavor. This claim, made carelessly by Hägglund, falls far short of being an accurate depiction of religious thought and life through the ages. Fervent religious hope for a temporal, effortful, constantly demanding afterlife is not at odds with intense striving for justice in this present life. It is a vision of the *continuation* of the challenges of such faithful and meaningful striving throughout unending time. I have even heard that there are rabbis who look forward to the task of endlessly discussing and debating with one another the inexhaustible truths of the Torah in the afterlife, as they have relished doing and have the charge of being responsible for doing in this life.

In the eighteenth century CE, the philosopher Immanuel Kant envisioned as a fundamental religious truth the idea—similar to the Jewish one just described—of the afterlife as a place where humans strive everlastingly for increasing approximations to the inexhaustible, forever challenging, and alluring Holy Will of God, knowing full well that, as finite creatures, they will never completely attain this goal (1960: 62). This life of earnest approximations thus takes place in time, not outside it. Kant's is a religious vision of an ongoing, demanding, purposeful life beyond the grave, not one of the negation of time or of life in time. Perpetual effort, not final rest and cessation of all effort, is the goal in this vision. If there is rest, it is only as temporary respite from work forever waiting to be accomplished.

So once again, it is not a necessary feature of all religious outlooks that they by nature ache for and aspire toward a timeless state of being, a supposed state of absolute quiescence and rest that I have argued to be neither desirable nor possible. Hägglund is clearly wrong in thinking this to be so and in maintaining that this idea marks the uncrossable dividing line between religious and secular conceptions of the nature and destiny of humankind. Kant's religious vision of an afterlife sees the afterlife as everlasting, not as timeless, and as regards humans in the afterlife as continuing to be finite, and finitely aspiring and developing, in their relations to the infinite holiness and perfection of God.

According to the contemporary Protestant and Roman Catholic theologians and biblical scholars John Dominic Crossan and Marcus Borg, respectively, preoccupation with the development and advancement of social justice in this present world is the overarching concern of the remarkable hymns of the Christmas story in the first two chapters of the Gospel of

Luke, namely, the *Magnificat*, the *Benedictus*, and the *Nunc Dimittis*, as well as of the Christmas stories in general and of the Jewish and Christian Bibles as a whole.

"The image of God's promise and of Jesus as a mighty savior," the two authors write, "concerns *this* world, not heaven" (Borg and Crossan 2009: 223). There is thus a strong continuity with the earlier Jewish earnest hope for a transformed world here on earth. Religion and politics, spirituality and a passion for this world are inseparable in the Advent story proclaimed by Matthew and Luke, according to the two contemporary Christian authors. "The God of the Bible is concerned about the whole of life," and that whole emphatically includes concern for social justice here-and-now, a concern that requires constant work on the part of human beings in partnership with a just, merciful, and loving God (223).

This outlook and injunction are not focused exclusively on life after death, on mere individual spirituality, or solely on the unaided work of God. It exhibits love for the world and gratitude for the opportunity to work with God for the world's ongoing transformation. Those with this outlook and conviction do not yearn simply to be freed from the present world and to leave it behind in a hope for a timeless or endless life to come beyond the grave. They yearn and feel charged by their religious faith to change this world for the good. So not only secular people are inspired by and exhibit in the course of their lives a passion for social justice. Hägglund is clearly wrong to assume that all religious people lack this passion in an alleged exclusive focus on a timeless (or endless) afterlife. There is much that is instructive and well worth pondering in his wide-ranging book, and I commend it strongly to the reader in other respects. But I must take issue with him on this one.

Problems with the Idea of an Everlasting Afterlife

We should also not fail to note that, *as finite*, the putatively resurrected and immortal humans are still subject to one of Hägglund's fundamental critiques that I made mention of earlier: faced with an infinite future, they will be sorely tempted to delay indefinitely the difficult, demanding decisions and actions required if they are to continue in a steady and perpetual process of personal approximation to the perfection of God's nature. Why not delay? There is no urgent need to put the shoulder to the wheel right away. Instead, infinite time stretches out before these immortal beings—

plenty of time to procrastinate and malinger without bad consequences. None of their mistakes in endless time is irreparable; there is ample time to make up for them and no need to worry about final unchangeability of their consequences. The lives and actions of Judaism's or Kant's resurrected beings will be in time and not timeless, but there will be no birth-to-death boundedness of time or relative brevity of earthly life to contend with or to feel urgent concern for.

We must therefore raise the serious question of whether such putatively immortal beings will be recognizably human or bear any resemblance to the kinds of finite beings they previously were in their time-bound lives on earth. Even with respect to this temporal but unending vision of an afterlife notably set forth by Jewish thinkers and Kant, I must agree with Hägglund's radical critique of religious visions of an afterlife as such. Whether timeless or endlessly temporal, they seem to me undesirable and implausible, and to a large extent for reasons such as those he adduces against them.

I also want to mention an additional reason for my personal rejection of the hope or need for either a timeless or endless afterlife in time. Everything known to us in this life or on this earth comes into being and passes away. As outcomes of biological evolution, there is no compelling reason to think that human beings are exempt from this observation. To think that all animals except human ones exist for a time and then cease to exist in the fulness of their times on earth is to claim an exceptional character for humans that sets them apart from every other creature or thing in nature. Our current modes of evolutionary and ecological thinking locate humans squarely within the natural order, not outside it.

Visions of a human afterlife set up an implausible hiatus between humans and nature, a hiatus that includes not only everything on earth that is fated someday to come to an end, but also the earth itself and in all probability every aspect of the present universe as a whole. To be is to be finite and to be caught up in the finitude of beginnings and endings. It is to come into being at one stage of existence and to cease to be at a later one. Time and matter-energy are, as I have argued elsewhere, primordial. All levels and kinds of reality here on earth and—as far as we can ascertain, everywhere else in the universe—have emerged and continue to do so from the creative as well as destructive interactions of these two codependent realities (Crosby 2020).

I have never heard or read a persuasive answer to the following question, and the question itself seems pointless to me: Why have we humans so often assumed that human life can be ultimately valuable, meaningful, or worthwhile *only if it lasts forever?* This assumption not only puts human beings at odds with everything else in nature, a nature where there could be no evolving creation of anything without destruction of something else—including destruction of the past moments of time in order that new ones can emerge—but that also rejects as ultimately tragic and even absurd a human life that is thought to end absolutely and forever at death.

Life lived in time and especially in the fulness of its normally allotted years, is something to be grateful for and not begrudged. It is a privilege to be allowed to live here on earth and, while we live, to be conscious participants in the evocative splendors of this world—even if it is only for a limited time. There is disappointment, tragedy, and regret—and sometimes even excruciating horror, pain, aimlessness, and loss—in our earthly lives, and this is sadly much truer of the lives of some persons and whole communities of persons than others. Some die early and have no opportunity to live a full and complete human life. The loved ones they leave behind are left to mourn their untimely passing. Some are born with serious physical or mental handicaps or suffer debilitating injuries at particular junctures of their lives. Some are less fortunate than others in numerous different ways, suffering, for example, gross injustice and mistreatment at the hands of other persons or because of flagrantly unjust institutions of society. There is tragedy and pain aplenty in earthly life and much of it is not subject to avoidance or remediation. The world in which we live is in many ways precarious and uncertain, marked by many tragic ambiguities.

However, the sheer fact of the boundedness of earthly life in time, its beginning in birth and ending at death, is not in itself a tragedy requiring resolution by some future unbounded existence. The point I want to make is that for something to be recognized as actually or potentially valuable and worthwhile, it does not have to last forever or be exempt from the conditions and constraints of temporal existence. It can be good and recognizably such over limited stretches of time and despite all of the threats and ambiguities of life in time. Suppose that Plato, Shankara, Dante, Shakespeare, Mahatma Gandhi, and other memorable historical figures did not finally escape the shackles of time or gain everlasting life: Would that make their lives ultimately meaningless or unimportant? Such a claim defies belief. As my wife Pam recently exclaimed about our cat Welby, lying stretched out luxuriously on his back on the screen porch floor: "What a wonderful world this one is, to have created such a marvelous creature!" We love him and rejoice in his existence. His life is of obvious importance to him and of inestimable value to us. And yet, we do not expect Welby to live forever.

To wish in dire times of severe anxiety, stress, disappointment, and sorrow that there be a timeless realm to which we humans can somehow escape is understandable and deserving of sympathy and compassion. But wishing does not make it so. The ultimate undesirability and incoherence of such a hope for such finite, time-bound creatures as humans militate against its being considered a meaningfully sought for and realizable option. The conception of it is in my judgment—as in that of Hägglund—susceptible to the kinds of fundamental criticism he and I feel compelled to mount against it.

I insist against Hägglund, then, that life in finite time can be unapologetically and fervently affirmed and affirmed *religiously*, with no promise or hope of an afterlife or prospect of some other kind of timeless or everlasting existence. In my view, such a temporally bounded life is, all things considered, inherently desirable and can be deeply admirable. I personally affirm its goodness and, indeed, its *sacredness*, and I do so with strongly felt and distinctively religious conviction—as I shall explain in the chapters to come. I take issue with Hägglund's claim that only secular people can as such make this affirmation, and that religious people never do. The difference between secular and religious outlooks and modes of life cannot be adequately drawn on this ground.

Conclusion

I have argued in this chapter that a timeless existence, and even an everlasting one, is in the last analysis undesirable, because it takes away so much of the character of our present lives as human beings. It radically dehumanizes us and renders us unrecognizable as the creatures we are in our present lives, with important tasks and concerns lying before us. As Martin Hägglund convincingly argues, a life outside of time, or even in infinitely extended time, would lose the fundamental human experiences of urgent, temporally pressing responsibility and care lived in the face of the inevitable but uncertain times of our impending death. Infinite rest or final release from care, whether in the form of an imagined timeless existence or in the form of an everlasting existence, is the negation not only of conceivable responsibility and care but of any compelling reason to continue to exist. As a consequence, it would be an empty life, one devoid of point or purpose.

There would be no use or need for such a life. It would either fail to allow for work of any kind or be lacking in motivation to work in timely fashion to contribute anything to the lives of particular human and nonhuman others or to the world as a whole. Working takes place in time, and we have no idea of how it would be possible outside of time or how it could continue to have compelling motivational force in infinite time. Thus, a timeless life or one infinitely extended in time would be a useless, superfluous, dilatory life—at least by any imaginable conditions of usefulness and urgent resolve known to us as finite creatures of time bounded by the adamant limits of birth and death.

A supposed life without time, either after death or within our present existence, is not conceivable. Timelessness or everlastingness runs counter to the radically and intimately time-bound character of everything in our experience as aspects of a world where all that exists comes into being and passes away, and where ongoing creation is made possible only by ongoing destruction. So fundamental is time to the character of the world and of ourselves as creatures of the world that we can gain no clear or commanding picture of what it would mean to exist outside of time or with infinitely extended, everlasting time.

It is not at all clear why we should think that human life can only be ultimately valuable and meaningful if it holds forth the hope of nontemporal or everlasting existence. We humans come into being at some particular point of time. We seem to have little difficulty accepting the idea that there once was a time when we did not exist. Why, then, should it be so shocking and unacceptable that our particular human lives, like everything else in the world, should ultimately cease to exist? We do not expect any other organic beings of nature to live forever. Why should we cling tenaciously to the idea that we human organisms, alone among all the rest of them, must have the prospect of escaping from the bonds of finite temporal existence in order to have ultimately valuable and meaningful lives?

Do our lives matter only if they go on forever or only if they can somehow break out altogether from the conditions, constraints, and boundaries of finite time? There would seem to be no convincing reason to give an affirmative answer to this question. I have sought to show in this chapter that there is in fact no such tenable or compelling reason to do so. Our days as human beings are numbered, but this unalterable fact does not in itself make them ultimately pointless, unfulfilled, or absurd. One can willingly and gratefully affirm this fact with stout religious faith and conviction, and there is no compelling need to grant Hägglund his contention that only secular-minded people or varieties of secular faith can consistently do so. We must look elsewhere for a more convincing way of distinguishing religious from secular ways of viewing and living in the world. I shall devote myself to this task in the remainder of this book.

Chapter Two

Fallible Human Knowledge

> The pride of the religiously devout is the most dangerous form of pride. There is a divisive pride of the learned, as well as of family wealth and power. The pride of those who feel themselves learned in the express and explicit will of God is the most exclusive. Those who have this pride, one that generates an exclusive institutionalism and then feeds and sustains itself through its connection with an institution claiming spiritual monopoly, feel themselves to be special organs of the divine, and in its name claim authority over others.
>
> —John Dewey (1960: 308)

In chapter 1, I showed that the distinction between religious and secular forms of faith cannot convincingly be drawn on the basis of their allegedly different views concerning time. It is not true that all religious traditions or all forms of religious faith allot—or must in their very nature allot—central importance either to the prospect of escaping from temporal existence altogether or to the promise of entering into a new kind of life with an unending future. Neither of these two beliefs is *essential* to genuine religious faith, although the two beliefs are admittedly prominent features of *some* types of religious faith. If not in this way, then, how should we go about distinguishing religion from secularity?

A second possible way is to assert that, while religious traditions and their adherents base their faith on claims to knowledge that are said to be certainly or absolutely true, secular outlooks and persons recognize only degrees of truth or probabilistic truths in all domains of thought. To be religious, then, is to cling to certain fundamental truth claims that are said to be inerrant and undeniable, while to be secular is to assert the fallibility or dubitable character of all basic claims to truth, including even the most fundamental claims made in the name of religion. However, this proposed way of trying to distinguish the religious from the secular will also not work, for reasons to be discussed in this chapter.

These reasons are four in number. First, no stated beliefs about realities of any sort—religious or otherwise—can convincingly transcend the fallibility of the human beings of any age who make claim to them. This observation pertains also to writers of the sacred scriptural texts of any given religious tradition.

Second, no human being can know what the future might bring in the way of any set of beliefs, religious or otherwise—no matter how indubitable, obvious, or incontestable such beliefs may seem to be at a particular time or even over long stretches of the past. Radical overturnings of both unquestioned secular and religious beliefs have occurred in the past, and there is no guarantee that such unexpected or even unimaginable overturnings will not occur in the future.

Third, claims to the infallibility or inerrancy of religious beliefs should be rejected because they erect insuperable barriers to any kind of ongoing, mutually enlightening interreligious or intrareligious dialogue or peaceful communal relationships. If I insist that my pivotal religious beliefs are absolutely true, then yours to the extent they differ fundamentally from mine must be absolutely false. Claims to the absolute truth of a particular set of religious convictions or of a particular religious tradition allow for no meaningful common ground. In the course of history, such claims have given sanction to disastrous tribalistic divisions, internecine conflicts, brutal colonial conquests, cruel pogroms, and oppressive injustices.

Fourth, a diversity of great religious traditions, each one with its basic commitments and beliefs, is both desirable and inevitable. It is desirable because each of these traditions is a facet on the elusive gem of religious truth, and it is inevitable because of the diverse perspectives and experiences of human cultures throughout human history. To make this observation is not to settle for a bland epistemological relativism in the field of religion, but it is to argue for attunement to different and yet often complementary ways of responding to profoundly important religious issues.

Secularists are well within their rights to oppose claims to the inerrancy of any religious scripture, tradition, doctrine, or belief. But they are mistaken if they also contend that this outlook is a necessary feature of religious faith and proceed to dismiss all forms of religious faith on this ground. One can assent to each of these four reasons and still have profound religious piety and conviction. In fact, acknowledgment of these reasons can contribute immeasurably to avoidance of such grave religious faults as the stubborn presumption and pride about which American philosopher John Dewey speaks in this chapter's epigraph, to say nothing of excluding from respect and inclusion all those who do not accept or willingly incorporate into their thought and practice a particular religious tradition's or group's claims to infallible certitude.

Frank acknowledgment of the fallibility of knowledge, belief, and conviction in all domains of thought—religious and otherwise—can rightly characterize both religious and secular outlooks on the world. Failure to do so on the part of some expressions of religious faith is not a basic difference of outlook that *universally* divides religion from secularity, although it admittedly *sometimes* does. Let us look in greater detail at each of the four routes to this acknowledgment that I have listed, in order to expose the inadequacy of the second alleged way of distinguishing between religious and secular forms of faith that is the focus of this chapter.

Fallibility of Human Claims to Truth

The thesis of this section is that all human claims to truth are fallible, meaning that they are at best partial and always open to question. This thesis applies to religious as well as to nonreligious claims wherever and whenever religious claims are set forth—whether in sacred texts, in ancient traditions, or by revered religious teachers. The unutterable holiness, unapproachable mystery, and radical indescribability of religious ultimates such as God, the Goddess, the gods, Brahman, the Dao, or the Buddha-nature in the great world religions stand adamantly in the way of their complete comprehension and description. Their realities can be felt and experienced but not finally characterized. Scriptures and traditions can point to these ultimates and do so in inspiring, informative ways, but they cannot provide absolute knowledge of them, and it is folly to insist that they can do so.

The great religious teachers are more often than not shrouded in the mists of time. Their teachings are steeped in assumptions, beliefs, and outlooks of their particular cultures and periods that may no longer be taken for granted, adhered to, or even fully understood in later times. These teachings, usually in originally oral rather than written form, are transmitted to us in writing by others, and by successive followers through time who claim (or are reported to claim) reliable transmissions of the teachers' lessons and examples. Applications of these teachings to the problems and concerns of a later time must be left to those of later times, opening room for legitimate differences of interpretation.

Furthermore, the great religious teachers' messages, as well as those of the sacred scriptures and traditions, are often couched in symbolic, metaphorical, mythological languages and in rituals, parables, stories, and koans whose possible meanings are difficult to comprehend or state. Their singular merit is their evocative suggestiveness and invitation to thought rather than exactitude of statement. As such, these meanings are often subject to tauntingly different interpretations and applications—even at the hands of the most competent and perceptive later interpreters. A variety of possibly complementary meanings stands in the stead of anything like a single absolute, clearly statable meaning or truth. The fallibility of human beings in religion as well as in all other areas of human thought is the backdrop of each of these observations.

In the two Western religions of Christianity and Islam, it has often been claimed that the respective scriptures of the two are inerrant in their every detail and thus the absolute guide in all matters of thought and practice. The seventeenth-century Lutheran theologian Johann Andreas Quenstedt, for example, insisted in his influential theological treatise that the Christian scriptures contain

> the infallible truth, free of any error; or to say the same thing in another way, in canonical Sacred Scripture there is no lie, no falsehood, not even the tiniest of errors [*nullus vel minimus error*], either in content or in words. Rather, each and every thing contained in it is altogether true, be it dogmatic or moral or historical, chronological, topographical, or onomastic. It is neither possible nor permissible to attribute to the amanuenses of the Holy Spirit any ignorance, lack of thought, or forgetfulness, or any lapse of memory, in recording Holy Writ. (Quenstedt, *Didactico-Polemical Theology*, as quoted in Pelikan 1984: 343–44)

The Holy Spirit is thus said to override and nullify any trace of human fallibility in every jot and tittle of the Christian scriptures, in its every reference, claim, name, or word. The writers of these scriptures are viewed as mere "amanuenses" or secretaries who faithfully take down divine *dictations* of infallible truths.

This idea is forcibly and unqualifiedly insisted upon by the twentieth-century Orthodox Presbyterian minister and founder of the Chalcedon

Foundation, Rousas John Rushdoony. The fall of human beings into sin as depicted in Genesis, he asserts, requires "an infallible Savior and an infallible Scripture," if there is to be any hope of the salvation of humans from the dread consequences of their state of sin. He elaborates this idea, saying that the Christian Bible "speaks to man with authority, and with sufficiency, that is, as a completed Word. It speaks with perspicuity, clearly and simply telling man who he is, what the nature of his sin is, what its remedy is and where it is to be found. The attributes of Scripture are thus necessity, authority, perspicuity, and sufficiency" (1995: 145).

Christian theologian and historian of ideas Francis A. Schaeffer exclaims that "the Bible tells men and women true things about God. Therefore, they can know true things about God. . . . That is, when God tells people what he is like, what he says is not just relatively true but absolutely true" (2005: 85–86). Schaeffer reiterates this position in another one of his works, telling us, "When I say Christianity is true I mean it is true to total reality—the total of what is, beginning with the central reality, the objective existence of the personal-infinite God. Christianity is not just a series of truths but *Truth*—Truth about all of reality" (1982: 19–20). Throughout his many writings, Schaeffer contrasts what he takes to be the absolute truths of the Bible with what he alleges to be the shifting, insecure relativities of truth claims and value commitments in contemporary culture.

In similar fashion, orthodox Muslims regard the Qur'an as the record of Allah's dictation, through the angel Gabriel, of his direct words to Muhammad—in a cave in Mecca—of the sūras or chapters of this sacred book. These words are said to be portions of a heavenly archetype transmitted to Muhammad in an Arabic version. As such, they are claimed to be absolutely true in every respect, and wholly without blemish or error. So once again, God as Holy Author is said to transmit inerrant truths through a body of scriptures communicated to human agency whose normal fallibility is transcended by unquestionable divine authority.

However, there are two prominent problems raised by the claim of absolute scriptural authority. One is the problem of how to safeguard correct interpretations of the sacred texts. Another is how to adapt them to changing times and circumstances. Over time, the question is bound to arise: What good does it do to claim absolute authority for these texts without a continuing, similarly authoritative protection of their reliable interpretations and applications? These two problems plagued proponents of the Protestant Reformation, with its central doctrine of *sola scriptura*, because it soon became clear that there was no inviolable consensus among Protestant leaders about how to interpret and apply a Bible that was said to contain inerrant truths in its every aspect. A good part of the Thirty Year's War in the seventeenth century was waged over this troublesome issue.

These problems also soon became serious ones in Islam, where appeal was made to the Hadith or traditional chain of companions of and successors to Muhammad after his death, in order to insure faithful and accurate interpretations and applications of the prophet's example, his teachings not contained in the Qur'an, and of the Qur'an itself. A similar move has long been made in Roman Catholic Christianity where a coequal or near-coequal authority has been claimed for the Church as the authoritative basis of the decision about what constituted the biblical canon (notably different in some respects from the Protestant canon) and as the guardian of proper interpretations and applications of its divinely revealed truths. The appeal to authoritative tradition was inevitable if the absolute authority of the sacred scriptures was to have practical meaning. And developing and maintaining the authority of tradition was a principal responsibility of the Church according to Roman Catholics. The nineteenth-century proclamation of the Pope's infallibility when speaking *ex cathedra* is consistent with assertion of the absolute authority of the Church as the guardian of sacred tradition.

Protestants also soon had to appeal to the authority of revered leaders such as Martin Luther, Huldrych Zwingli, John Calvin, John Knox, and Menno Simons in order to wend a reliable way through a cacophony of voices as the Reformation widened, each claiming to have its own definitive interpretations and applications of the Protestant Bible. A similar problem erupted with the spread of Islam and its division into Sunni, Shiite, and Sufi interpretations and applications of the Qur'an.

The nineteenth-century movement called Biblical Criticism posed another problem for the claim to its literal inerrancy. The Bible was studied in ways similar to the study of other ancient texts. Its historical settings and circumstances were analyzed in great detail. Questions about its stages of transmission and development were posed. The variant readings of the biblical text in available manuscripts and translations were subjected to scrutiny. The cultural assumptions and beliefs of biblical times were compared with those of later times. It became apparent to many Protestant and Catholic Christians that the Bible is far from being a unitary monologue dictated by God to human secretaries. Instead, it is an anthology of writings developed over a thousand-year period and preceded in many instances by oral and written stages of development that were in some ways notably different in character.

Variant readings in ancient manuscripts and in the many different translations of the Bible, to say nothing of the question of which ancient texts constitute legitimate parts of the Bible, forced nineteenth-century theologians such as Alexander Hodge and Benjamin Warfield to claim that the absolute authority of the Bible resides only in its "original autographs" (or writings) and not in any of its current versions. But of course these putative original autographs are no longer available and constitute only what one historian has called an "imaginary Bible" (FitzGerald 2017: 78–79). The absolute authority of a *nonexistent Bible* is thin gruel as a basis for a lifetime of religious faith.

Judaism has had its own struggles regarding the authority of the Hebrew Bible and the credibility and legitimacy of its duly recognized rabbinic interpreters, the latter called exponents of the "oral Torah" as contrasted with the biblical Torah in its written form. Here is how the Jewish writer Bernard J. Bamberger poses the issue of the respective authorities of the Bible and its learned interpreters in the first and second centuries CE:

> It must be remembered that, to the Rabbis, the Torah was a document of supernatural perfection, and they naturally expected that all good ideas would be found there—at least by way of suggestion. A system of interpretation drawn up by Hillel and enlarged by R. Ishmael in the second century [CE], treated the Torah as a document speaking in human terms, whose implications are to be derived by logical reasoning. But another viewpoint, upheld by Ishmael's great opponent Akiba, insisted that there was not a superfluous letter in the text, and read special meanings into every "if," "but," and "and." (1964: 110)

Akiba's position regarding the Torah reminds us of Catholic and Protestant appeals to an allegedly infallible Christian Bible, while Hillel's and Ishmael's views exhibit the need for ongoing interpretations of the Torah's meanings and of its applications to the issues of their time. Bamberger notes that an important Jewish group at this time was the Sadducees, "who opposed the whole idea of the oral Torah, which they attacked as unscriptural and consequently invalid. The Rabbis were thus at pains to find as far as possible a Biblical basis for the oral teachings" (110). The conservative Sadducees rejected, for example, the idea of the afterlife on the ground that it was not set forth in the written Torah, while the more liberal Pharisees accepted it as an important Jewish belief that had come to the fore following upon the period after the return from the exile into Babylon when most of the Hebrew Bible had been rendered into written form. Similar controversial issues arose early on in the history of Islam, and response to it was the development and appeal to the Hadith as a supplemental authority to the Qur'an.

The Pharisaic view won out in Judaism for the most part, and the Sadducee's outlook—akin in some ways to that of Christian and Muslim conservatives who counseled strict restriction to literal biblical or Qur'anic authority—became less influential. I think that the Pharisees were right to take issue with the conservative Sadducees in this way, because without ongoing interpretation, application, and supplementation of sacred texts, these texts would not only become increasingly at odds with changing times. Their culturally dated or after a certain time vague or incomplete statements and references would soon cease to have any palpable religious significance. Such scriptural passages might continue to be recited but would no longer be understood or meaningfully incorporated into the religious life.

The history of the Hebrew Bible's development over at least ten centuries testifies in and of itself to a changeable and developing *biblical tradition*. And while the Qur'an reached its present form thanks to the reports of one man in one century, the prophet Muhammad, it too required for its continuing religious relevance and use the supplementations of Hadith and Sharia (written religious law). Of course, active, ongoing interpretation and application of sacred texts also pose the risks of misinterpretation and misapplication. There is no escape from human fallibility or error, as I am emphasizing throughout this chapter. A similar lesson could be learned from the histories of religions other than Judaism, Christianity, and Islam. Examples ready at hand are the Dao that cannot be spoken and Brahman without qualities (Nirguna Brahman). Neither can be reduced to or adequately described by a set of infallible statements or descriptions.

In all of the respects indicated in this section, the fallibility of humans and of all of their works and claims—scriptural, traditional, secular, or otherwise through the centuries—is inescapably evident. It is readily acknowledged by many religious thinkers today. They stoutly affirm the cherished inspiration and guidance of sacred texts and traditions but feel no need to insist on their infallible truth or on the infallible truths of any of their own personal commitments and beliefs. Their rejection of inerrancy as a necessary feature of their faith does not automatically make them *secular* in thought and practice. It allows them to be humbly but fully and unapologetically religious.

Thus it is demonstrably possible to have firm and deeply meaningful religious faith without asserting absolute, indefeasible authority for any of the beliefs associated with a particular form of faith. In my view, the most faithful and perceptive kind of religious sensibility involves continuing openness to and active interest in the different and sometimes radically different religious convictions of others. There is much to be pondered and learned religiously in this way. But a mutual acknowledgment of human fallibility is necessary if such dialogue is to have this effect. I discuss this important point in the fourth section below.

Unknowability of Future Beliefs

A final implacable barrier to the tenability of a claimed infallibility of any set of beliefs, whether religious or secular, is the openness of the future. Revolutionary new ways of thinking, feeling, or acting are revolutionary precisely because they were not predictable or even conceivable at an earlier time. The two scientific revolutions, first in the seventeenth century and then again in the twentieth century, are cases in point. At present, our scientific beliefs and attitudes toward the world are generally in keeping with the second scientific revolution. But who can claim entirely dependable knowledge of what the future might bring in the way of radically new ways of conceiving and responding to scientific problems?

The second scientific revolution came as a shock to those living and thinking within the mostly unquestioned framework of the first one. There was an abruptness about this second revolution, despite its being vaguely prefigured by some earlier developments or anomalies of the regnant scientific thought of the earlier time. It is at least possible, if not probable, that a third scientific revolution is lurking behind the scenes of the second one, and that it will make its entrance onto the stage of history with similar abruptness and present unpredictability.

We should not fail to note that the very conception of natural science that we presently take for granted was the fruit of the first scientific revolution's blending of increasingly precise empirical observations made possible by new instruments such as Galileo Galilei's telescope, together with increasingly precise mathematical description, much of the latter made possible by new kinds of mathematical investigation and formulation such as those introduced by René Descartes's analytical geometry and Gottfried

Leibniz's and Isaac Newton's calculus. None of this was completely without precedent, but the novel reconceptualizations of existing knowledge and experience, supplemented by many fresh observations, discoveries, and methods, were—taken as a whole—radically unexpected at the time. They were even thought to be bizarre and entirely unacceptable by some thinkers of the time, and especially by many religious thinkers.

Similarly, there is no way to be sure that a new Galileo, Newton, Max Planck, or Albert Einstein will not usher in a radically different kind of science at some point in our own future. Awareness of this distinct possibility guards against assuming that present ways of scientific thinking are infallible and immune to change—no matter how perspicuous, inviolable, undeniable, or elegant they may seem to be at any given time. The lesson of ongoing history tells a quite different story.

Similar stories could be told of the histories of art, morality, politics, technology, philosophy, and whole civilizations. Nowhere in any of these domains is there a demonstrable immunity to fundamental changes of outlook, style, method, or content. How, then, could it be conceivably different for the history of religions? An unbiased look at the history of all religions reveals ongoing development, reconstitution, and change. Religious claims to truth are no less moving targets than are claims in any other fields of thought and experience. All are outcomes of fallible human quests, experiences, outlooks, and conceptualizations. And all are profoundly influenced by their surrounding cultures and times. This being the case, there is no way to cordon off religious beliefs from possible change or from changes that may be unimagined or even unimaginable at a particular time.

Moreover, there is no way to preempt the possibility of *new religions* emerging, just as they have emerged in the past. These new religions may have a significantly unanticipated character, as Buddhism did when it emerged from the womb of Hinduism, Christianity when it came out of the seedbed of Judaism, or Islam when it claimed to continue and complete a process of divine revelation already begun in Judaism and Christianity.

Religious claims to infallible, unchangeable truths are shattered on the rock of unceasing historical development and change. The continuing openness to the novelty of an unknowable future makes all such claims untenable, no matter how ardently and piously assertions of their timeless or time-transcending truths may be insisted upon. Defeasible truths in all aspects of all fields of thought, including the field of religion, are unavoidable. The fallibility of the human subjects in those fields of thought cannot be excised from their most confident proclamations.

But what about the idea that the proclamations of sacred texts—or at least the most central and vital ones—are forever guarded from error by their divine origin or by some other claimed sacred origin and insurance of absolute truth? This claim is one invariably made by fallible humans as well. It is human interpretation of the character, value, and meaning of a sacred text. There is no way around the fact of essential human involvement in all such claims. All attempts to find a short cut to the sacred or to sacred texts that eliminate corrigible human involvements in their original forms of presentation, as well as in subsequent responses to and interpretations of these original forms, are doomed to failure. Such attempts must convincingly fail in light of the uncertainty and unknowability of the future. Being religious does not require that one fly in the face of these stubborn facts, despite the insistence of some religious defenders of textual and other kinds of religious infallibility that it is in exceptional cases both possible and necessary to do so.

American philosopher William James addresses this issue with convincing clarity and force. He does so in his 1891 essay "The Moral Philosopher and the Moral Life," where he examines the similar notion of absolute *moral values* that have been claimed by many thinkers to exist in timeless priority to our discoveries of them in our temporal thought and experience, and that are asserted by these thinkers to be the necessary source and support of these values if they are to have binding authority on our fallible lives. Such putative absolute moral values, James notes, can take the forms of *synthetic a priori* principles (principles that are necessarily true and implicit in and applicable to all empirical situations having moral character or posing moral problems), or of values eternally envisioned in the overarching infallible consciousness of God. He dismisses this view from consideration, just as I am arguing we ought to dismiss the notion of a necessary infallibility of religious scriptures, religious traditions, or great religious teachers. The alleged infallibility of either moral principles or religious claims means nothing if ways are not found to test and affirm them as valuable and true in our own experience and to incorporate them into our individual and social lives.

But—and here is the crux of the matter—the principles and claims become *inescapably fallible* once they are subjected, and in the nature of the case must necessarily be subjected, to this kind of test if they are to have meaning for finite beings such as we undeniably are. So we can readily *dispense* with appeals to or the need for absolute values, necessary truths, and every kind of allegedly infallible idea or principle—moral, religious, or otherwise—once we understand that values and truths can have meaning only when they are recognized as always initially tentative and only subsequently, if at all, appropriated and affirmed by the continuing experiences and investigations of our fallible consciousnesses and finite selves. James puts the point this way:

> A claim thus livingly acknowledged is acknowledged with a solidity and fulness which no thought of an "ideal" backing can render more complete; while if, on the other hand, the heart's response is withheld, the stubborn phenomenon is there of an impotence in the claims which the universe [allegedly] embodies, which no talk about an eternal nature of things can gloze over or dispel. An ineffective a priori order is as impotent a thing as an ineffective God. . . . (1977: 618)

I have to agree strongly with James that the fallible processes of empirical interpretation, incorporation, and testing by beings such as ourselves cannot be overruled or made unnecessary by some kind of a priori principle or source, or by claims purporting to represent the infallible perspective of God or some other kind of sacred guarantor.

Acceptance of this observation about human fallibility is indispensable for religious dialogue because it requires admission at the outset of the susceptibility to error, and capability of only partial religious truth at best, of all participants in such dialogues, whatever their respective religious commitments might be.

Dangers of Claims to Infallible Religious Beliefs

Claims to the infallibility of particular religions or religious teachings are not always innocuous. They can occasion bitter controversies and bloody wars. This is especially true when eternal salvation, peaceful social order, or viable civilization is believed to hang on the truth of such claims. One religion's infallibility is another's grave error, when both claim infallibility for particular claims that are fundamentally inconsistent with or differ from another. If both claim to speak in the name of the sacred or divine, and when the respective social orders and fundamental cultural outlooks of the two are based on or intricately interwoven with such claims, compromise on important matters is impossible and conflict is unavoidable. Each group's insistence on the infallibility of its central but fundamentally different outlooks and beliefs stands obstinately in the way of peaceful resolution of their disagreements and disputes.

Wars have sometimes been fought within and not just between or among nations when different constituencies of those nations make different claims to religious absoluteness. The bitter battles between Protestants and Catholics, or between Oliver Cromwell's Puritan followers and defenders of the Crown and its Established Anglican Church in seventeenth-century England and Scotland, as well as combats between Catholics and Protestants in twentieth-century Ireland, illustrate this point. The Thirty Years' War in seventeenth-century Europe was fought to a significant extent over different claims to infallible religious truth, both between Roman Catholic and Protestant groups and within those groups. The perennial clashes in the Balkan countries, where Catholic, Orthodox, Protestant, and Islamic parties are involved, provide another out of numerous such examples. To them we can add the conflicts between Hindus and Muslims in India and Hindus and Buddhists in Sri Lanka—conflicts with religious as well as secular roots.

Absolutistic, wholly inflexible and unyielding claims to religious truth are by no means the sole sources of such conflicts, but they often play a central role, whether consciously or unconsciously. Differences among religious beliefs have often come to be seen as intractable and nonnegotiable, not only within or among particular religious institutions and their practitioners, but also within and among the nations where they have played a dominant role. Claims to the infallibility or indisputable truth of the respective religions' basic beliefs have long been a prominent factor in the inability of nations, institutions, and peoples to get along with one another. The rise of the secular state, now so common to many of the states of the world, has been motivated largely by this amply demonstrated historical fact. A secular state is charged with refusing to give priority to any one religious tradition while allowing different ones to flourish.

We can add to these observations indication of what happens when one state assumes the right to conquer, dominate, and colonize other states on the ground that it has the infallible religious right and even duty to do so. This is a sad and familiar story of history. The brutal and even genocidal Jewish conquest of parts of Canaan that is nevertheless celebrated in the Hebrew Bible, the Muslim conquests sweeping from Arabia to Spain and to the east as well, the European conquests and decimations of aboriginal groups in the Americas and elsewhere, and the British conquests of other peoples for the announced purpose of advancing Christian civilization throughout the world, are all examples of this phenomenon.

An instructive example of the kind of intrareligious dispute that can take place, and of the damage that can be done to human lives by appeals to supposedly infallible sources in such disputes, is the contentious wrangling in the worldwide United Methodist Church at the time of this writing over the issue of whether professed and practicing same-sex persons should be allowed to marry or be candidates for ordination as ministers in the denomination's churches. So-called traditionalists contend that the issue can be settled simply by consulting appropriate texts in the Bible, because the Bible is the infallible words of God. They cite a few texts from Leviticus, one from Romans, and a few others in defense of their view that professed and practicing same-sex persons should not be allowed to participate in the full life of the church, including marriage and ordination, because the Bible prohibits it. There is no need for further discussion or adjudication.

Methodist inclusivists or progressives insist, on the other hand, that the issue cannot be decisively settled in this fashion. They make this claim on the ground that however fervently the Bible should be revered as a sacred text it is a mistake to view it as timelessly infallible. A lot has happened in the two-thousand years since the Bible came to be a written text, and these changes should be taken into account. For example, the ancient writers of the biblical period knew nothing about the science of genetics and as a consequence could not recognize the distinct possibility if not strong probability that some people are genetically disposed to same-sex relations just as others, who happen to be in the majority, are disposed to heterosexual ones. The former's sexual disposition may not be a matter of mere choice and therefore cannot be regarded simply as some kind of deliberately decided perversity or sin. Furthermore, same-sex professions and practices should not be branded, in this view, as abhorrent and sinful just because they are different. For the progressives or inclusivists who take this position, same-sex people should be allowed to participate in every aspect of the life of the church just as heterosexual people currently are.

The resolution of this current problem confronting the United Methodist Church, the progressives contend, does not lie in an external, putatively infallible document but in the considered judgments of contemporary Methodists, judgments recognizing that the views of ancient folk, even of those involved in the writings of sacred texts, are not absolute determinants for all time of what should be believed and practiced by Christians living today. The alleged infallibility of such writings must be rejected because they have to be interpreted and applied to in the present, and apart from such interpretations and applications they would have no viable relevance or meaning for today's world.

Moreover, to claim that these writings are infallible is already to subject them to interpretation and application, and to do so as fallible human beings. So-called *literal* readings of the Bible are themselves debatable *interpretations* of its meanings. Laying claim to a sacred text's putative infallibility and putting it to use in this fashion is one kind of interpretation and application among others. The claim cannot circumvent subjection to the necessary filter of fallible and possibly differing human judgments, a filter without which, as we witnessed William James to argue concerning any and all useful moral values, the sacred text could have no meanings for human life. The ardent cry "The Bible says" does not automatically eliminate the need for further discussion or make unnecessary contemporary considerations, interpretations, and applications. In view of what has been said elsewhere in this chapter, it should be clear that I side with the progressive thinkers who take this view.

The Bible can be reverenced for its wisdom, but it should not be slavishly, unthinkingly cited and obeyed. Rightly regarded, it is a living document, not a dead letter. Appeal to a few select passages does not close off discussion but should be set within the context of the Bible's times and within the context of its overall spirit and message. When the latter is conscientiously done, the example and teaching of *all* of the Torah, the Hebrew prophets, and the Jesus of the Gospels must be taken fully into account. Welcoming inclusion of the weak, the poor, the widows and orphans, the ostracized, the different, and the strangers at the gate is a pervasive biblical motif that should be set in contrast with the idea that professing and practicing same-sex people should be peremptorily prohibited from participation in aspects of the church's life.

The hurt, shame, and sense of rejection inflicted on these fellow humans is a high price to pay—and much too high a price at that—for blind obedience to a few ancient prohibitions, even when the latter are contained in the Holy Bible. So once again, stubborn appeals to allegedly infallible external sources, with no allowance for further thought and investigation, can be more destructive than helpful so far as the peace of intrareligious relationships and the judicious progress of institutional policies are concerned. One can forcefully reject the finality of such appeals in *an avowedly religious* and *not merely secular* spirit. Fallible appraisal and adjudications of differing views will always be required. Biblical passages relating to sexuality and other controversial topics must be brought to the tests of current human judgment by thoughtful Christians to see if they can be rightly affirmed in the world of today as being "of God" (I John 4:1).

Inevitable and Desirable Religious Diversity

In this final section, I argue that religious diversity is not only inevitable but also highly desirable. It is inevitable for a number of reasons. One of them is that, as I have sought to show, above, there can be no such thing as infallibility of statement, belief, or principle, whether in the area of religion or in any other spheres of human experience and thought, that automatically confers supremacy on any religious outlook. A variety of religious scriptures, traditions, teachers, and worldviews reflects the fallible judgments about religious concerns that have been made throughout human history and that continue to be made today. No religious tradition is exempt from such fallibility, meaning that no one tradition can convincingly claim absolute priority of faith and doctrine over all the others.

Human cultures as a whole, including their religious aspects, are conspicuously different from one another despite the fact of their evident similarities in certain basic respects. For example, all cultures must take careful, constant account of the human need for food, water, shelter, and procreation, and of the need for enough commonality of assumption, belief, and practice to make possible a relatively peaceful and stable social existence. Cultures achieve these goals in a remarkable variety of ways, and their respective religious beliefs and practices are no less variable and different. Each of the latter speaks to the irrepressible human need for overarching purpose, value, and meaning, that is, for orientation, direction, and guidance for the whole of life. The various religious traditions take account not only of the human need for the physical resources necessary for life, but also of the historically attested and ever-present human need to have some things fundamentally worth living for. This need involves reasons for being that can provide courage to persevere in the face of life's formidable threats and uncertainties, courage conferred by profound existential meanings capable of challenging, enriching, rejuvenating, and sustaining the entire span of a person's life.

Each religious tradition does so in its own distinctive fashion. Secular forms of faith can also perform this function, and they also do this in markedly different ways. Whether religious or secular, the inescapability of different long-established, deeply influential cultural frameworks—along with the unavoidable fallibility of both religious and secular worldviews and ways of life—stand as insuperable barriers to the prospect of any one cultural system having the right to exercise final dominance over all of the others or of an ultimate hegemony of any single type of religious or secular faith. An endless, ever-changing cultural variety and a ceaseless diversity of forms of faith are in all probability inevitable, because neither the former nor the latter is amenable to some kind of finally determinant infallible judgments, either of the present or of the conceivable future. Large-scale cultural forms of life are fallible and changeable over time, as history clearly shows. The same is by all evidence true of any culture's constituent religious and secular forms of faith.

I also believe that an ineliminable variety of the great religious traditions of the world should be welcomed and cherished. None should try to eclipse the others, and their different forms should all be allowed to flourish to the extent that each one promulgates an evocative, just, and supportive religious vision. Allowance for the free expressions of diverse kinds of religious faith can be sources of harmony and accord, and their interactions can be spurs to the continual reexamination, enhancement, and improvement of each one of them. False claims to infallibility can only arrest this highly desirable process.

The British philosopher Alfred North Whitehead's conception of a "harmony of contrasts" is applicable here (see Whitehead 1958: 86; 1967: 267–68, 282–83). Each diverse and contrasting manifestation of the religious aspiration—like the separate but mutually contributory parts of a work of art—can adumbrate in its own limited fashion an imagined but never to be finally achieved whole truth and meaning of religion that no one of them exhaustively captures or conveys. From the inspiration and lure of this imagined and ever-beckoning, but never to be achieved whole truth of religion, each religious tradition earns its entitlement to serious attention and to instructive and evocative religious significance.

No stale sameness of outlook or tame conformity of practice can match the variegated pattern of enticingly different perspectives among the great world religions. Claims to the infallibility of any one religious tradition can only short-circuit this alluring vision of the whole. A plurality of religions, each with its admittedly fallible claims to truth, accomplishes what a single religion by itself never could. Recognition and affirmation of this inevitable fallibility has profound religious importance. It is therefore fallacious and misleading for proponents of secular faith to think that only their perspectives—and no genuinely religious ones—can readily acknowledge and declare the fallibility of all claims to truths, including truths of faith.

In making these important observations, I do not mean to imply that all of the world religions are equally true or that they equally approximate to the ideal of final religious truth. I do not need to address this issue here. I only mean to say that each one has important and even indispensable contributions to make to religious understanding from its own fallible perspective, and that persistent engagement and dialogue among them should be welcomed and encouraged. Religious truth can be enlarged in this way, and enlarged to a significant extent. But it will never be finally achieved or made perfect. The fallibility of all religious outlooks, systems, and traditions should not be seen as a defect but as an opportunity. Recognition of it can function as a lure to deeper investigation and understanding for each religious tradition, a lure that seeks out as many available resources as possible for the continuing development and expansion of its distinctive vision. Prominent among such resources are what can be learned and needs to be learned from the religious experiences, conceptions, symbols, and practices that are centrally important to the other religions of the world.

Conclusion

I have argued in this chapter that religious texts, traditions, outlooks, and beliefs are no less fallible and debatable in their every respect than are secular ones. Therefore, the distinction between religion and secularity cannot be convincingly drawn in this manner any more than it can be made on the basis of their alleged respective views of time—the focus of the first chapter.

It remains true, however, that proponents of religious systems have sometimes and even frequently throughout history laid claim to the infallibility or inalterability of their central texts and doctrines. I have sought to show that this claim runs up against two *descriptive* obstacles and two *prescriptive* ones. The descriptive ones are related to recognizable matters of fact, while the prescriptive ones are intended to display the crucial desirability of acknowledging the fallibility of all religious claims to truth including one's own if one professes such, and of being willing to enter into frank and open-minded dialogue with those whose personal convictions and perspectives differ from one's own.

The first descriptive obstacle is the inescapable fallibility of human beings, demonstrably evident in the field of religion as well as in all other areas of human thought. Even if sacred *scriptures* are claimed to be infallible, their infallibility means little or nothing in the final analysis, given the fact that they can have useful value and meaning only when interpreted and applied by fallible humans. Sacred texts must be brought down to earth, so to speak, when applied within the constraints of changing cultures and changing times, and when applied to circumstances and problems not anticipated or explicitly addressed in the texts. Their imagined infallibility turns out to have no practical meaning or use.

Attempts to safeguard the infallibility of the sacred texts with claims to equally infallible religious *traditions* pose the same intractable problem in a different guise. The different interpretations, prioritizations, and readings of both texts and traditions that inevitably crop up in the histories of religious communities add further evidence of unavoidable human fallibility. When the sacred scriptures themselves are present only in different extant versions, appeals to their currently nonexistent original forms exposes the practical futility of unquestioning reliance on the texts' supposed infallibility. Whatever outlook or worldview continues to be applied and put to human use in a world of changing cultures and changing times is going to be unavoidably fallible and subject to different points of view.

The second descriptive obstacle to believable assertion of the infallibility of any system of belief and practice, including religious ones, is the obstinate fact of an open, unknowable future and especially of the relatively distant future. The future is replete with unpredictable surprises, as even a superficial study of history unmistakably shows. What seem to be the fixed, obvious, undeniable truths in one age may no longer be credible or come to be seen as the quaint, obsolete, or even risible curiosities of a later age. The two revolutions of scientific thought in the recent history of the West make this point clear. The first made many long-cherished aspects of ancient and medieval thought no longer credible, and the second revolution cast into doubt some central assumptions and theories of the previously dominant and widely assumed Newtonian science. What present guarantee can be provided that no *third* scientific revolution, unimaginable at present, looms over the horizon of the near or more distant future?

In similar fashion, radical alternatives to particular religious outlooks and perspectives may surprise us in the future just as they have in the past. The future may introduce unexpected forms of religiosity within existing religious traditions and give birth to astonishingly altered religious systems, bold new interactions of current religious systems, and unprecedented ways of thinking and acting religiously. History does not stand still. The unpredictability of the future is decisive indication of the fallibility of humans in all domains of their thought and experience. One can be deeply religious while readily acknowledging the murkiness of what is yet to occur in the relentless passage of time, a murkiness that is likely to become increasingly impenetrable as it extends further and further into the future. We creatures of time are forever subject to the uncertainties of the future.

The two prescriptive analyses of commitment to the infallibility of particular religious teachings are, first, fervent opposition to the barrier erected by such claims against the possibility of constructive, fruitful dialogue either within particular religious traditions or between and among different religious traditions. The tragic outcomes of this barrier are exhibited in the sad histories of brutal interreligious warfare and in unyielding intrareligious conflicts that have turned to a significant degree on differing tenacious claims to infallibility and have often torn religious communities apart. The barrier erected by stubborn and implausible insistences on infallibility ought to be dismantled for the sake of social harmony and a peaceful, mutually instructive cooperation of religious groups.

The second prescriptive analysis emphasizes the inevitability but also the inestimable value of a diversity of religious traditions and the high desirability of frequently initiated and ongoing dialogues among adherents of religious traditions. This emphasis is especially important in our currently shrinking world, with its increasingly necessary interactions of different peoples and cultures. Failure to acknowledge either the inevitability of religious differences or the desirability of increasing interactions among peoples with different kinds of religious faith is the height of folly, especially when it is based on unyielding even though demonstrably untenable claims to religious infallibility.

Adherents of the various forms of religious faith and exponents of various secular versions of faith can join hands in giving urgent emphasis to the pressing need for constructive religious as well as secular interactions. Sustained critiques of claims to infallibility of any imagined kind should function as an essential religious and secular duty and should be conceived as an indispensable way of helping to bring adherents of different religious or secular faiths into respectful dialogue with one another rather than plunging them into intractable opposition. Candid recognition and exploration of religious differences can be mutually challenging and enlightening, and need not be unsettling or disruptive. They can expand and deepen religious sensibility and awareness rather than threatening it. The same point applies to secular disputes. These too can become unduly disruptive or even violent when disputants believe themselves to be possessed of indubitable truths of one kind or another. Claims to religious or secular kinds of absolute epistemic certainty exhibit an unyielding human pride and are implacable enemies of progress and peaceful accord. There is no warrant for assuming that only secular-minded people are willing to acknowledge and affirm this crucial truth.

Chapter Three

Science, Secularity, and Religion

> Religions, whether they venture upon internal programs of secularization within themselves or not, confront the unyielding fact that, increasingly, they exist in and participate in secular societies. They not only have to do with secular governments, they confront a climate of opinion and judgment which tends to be answerable more to the findings of the sciences than to the teachings of religion or the reflections of philosophers. Science, in fact, has assumed an ascendency in our time that is unprecedented in the history of civilization.
>
> —Bernard Eugene Meland (1966: 147)

As Christian theologian Bernard Meland notes in the epigraph to this chapter, all religious traditions are being exposed more and more in recent times to the influences of secular cultures, and especially to the powerful influences of the natural and social sciences. In consequence, religious references to supernatural realms, presences, powers, and truths are eliciting increasing levels of skepticism and doubt. What cannot be brought within the scope of scientific inquiry and explanation, many claim in today's world, is bogus and unreal, and thus unworthy of investigation or discussion.

For those who take this view of the difference between religion and secularity, a sensitivity guided by the spirit, methods, and approaches of the sciences is the most promising route to truth in all areas of thought and experience. They allege that this route is thoroughly secular in character and requires no reference or appeal to any sort of distinctively religious tradition, symbolism, teaching, or vision. Secularism, or staunch *resistance to all things religious* by this interpretation of religion's character, is thus seen as the only trustworthy basis for understanding ourselves and the world we inhabit. Religions are to be set aside as hopelessly mired in nonscientific, old-fashioned, now-outmoded ways of thinking and experiencing.

To be religious is by its very nature—according to this view—to be committed to unsupported, unsupportable, and even preposterous beliefs in some kind of unscientific, unearthly, unnatural, immaterial reality thought to exist beyond the reach of the five senses and the range of our ordinary experiences, as well as outside of mundane nature. According to this growingly influential type of thinking, secularism's uncompromising rootedness in and restriction to the *natural* world should be set in strict opposition to religion's commitment to supposed *supernatural* spheres and types of existent. A scientifically minded secular outlook urges us to put the religious past firmly behind us and to devote all of our thoughts, energies, and aspirations to a scientifically guided secular future. Religion is a thing of the past; scientific ways of responding to our lives in the world are the irrepressible wave of the future.

In chapter 1, I argued against the idea that religion can be distinguished from secularism on the basis of the two stances' alleged fundamentally different views of time. In chapter 2, I criticized the idea that the two outlooks can be distinguished by maintaining that religion relies necessarily on presumed infallible truths, while secularism rests on the conviction that all truths are fallible and therefore susceptible to question and to possible refutation.

In this chapter I critically discuss a third way of seeking to draw a sharp line between religion and secularism. This is the view that all forms of religion are predominantly supernatural in their dependence on and references to *otherworldly* revelations and realities, while secular forms of faith are committed to the proposition that the only reliable truths and references are those open to scientific methods of verification or falsification—and that are grounded solely *in this world* and in the mundane experiences and judgments of human beings. Those who take this position argue that appeals to supernatural sources of meaning and truth, or to supernatural realms and beings, are fanciful and no longer credible in a scientific age. They contend that religious ways of thinking and acting should give way to secular ones and observe that these older religious ways of thinking are being seen as increasingly untenable and unconvincing throughout the world in our present scientific and technological age.

The latter is an empirical claim that shall not occupy me here. The focus of my discussion in this chapter is on two allegations. The first one is that religion by its very nature rests on grounds of supernatural authority rather than scientific reasoning for its basic affirmations, and the second one is that religion, *qua* religion, necessarily makes basic references to supernatural realms, beings, occurrences, and powers. Religion therefore differs in these two fundamental respects from secular ways of thinking. This way of distinguishing religion and secularity is admittedly applicable to many types of religious faith, but it does not apply to all types. Therefore, it does not constitute a convincing way of drawing the basic distinction. This is the proposition I discuss and defend in the present chapter. In doing so, I provide reasons for rejecting the proposed third way of drawing a categorical distinction between religious and secular outlooks, or between what I shall later refer to as the sacred and the secular.

In the first section of this chapter, I argue that religion has a great deal to learn from science and should, whenever appropriate, adjust, expand, or modify its teachings in light of what it learns. Religion as I view it is not something fixed in place or staying the same throughout all time. Properly regarded, it is dynamic and ever responsive to change, and in this way it seeks always to be relevant to the cultures of changing times. Religion is therefore not opposed to science or to scientific developments of its time but is at its best deeply responsive to science and to other sources of fresh insight and perspective wherever these are to be found. I speak prescriptively here, but I also argue that this close relationship to science and to other aspects of contemporary culture is a factual way of describing those religious persons, groups, and traditions of our day that continue to be open to changing circumstances and changing times—and especially to the findings of current science. There is no reason to think, therefore, that religion must by its nature be opposed to science or to all or most other aspects of contemporary culture, and no compelling reason to interpret the distinction between religion and secularism on this basis.

In the second section, I focus on the restricted scope of science and in this way resist the idea that it should have a hegemonic relation to other aspects of culture, including the religious aspects. Religion has a distinctive cultural role that science cannot fulfill and should make no effort to fulfill. It would be folly to think of science as having the ability to eclipse and make unnecessary the roles of art, morality, philosophy, or other humanistic perspectives, and it makes no more sense to think of science as replacing religion or taking over whatever is legitimate in it and leaving the rest behind.

There are aspects of current religious attitudes and beliefs, and especially in some religious quarters, that run directly counter to particular dictums of science, and these should be reconsidered, revised, and, if need be, set aside. But the whole of religious vision, meaning, and truth cannot be convincingly swallowed up into a science that has the temerity to claim dominance or veto power over all things religious. Religion is right to resist hegemonic science, that is, the idea that all that is of value and importance in religion can be explained, accounted for, and handled more competently and persuasively by science. Every basic aspect of culture has its appropriate role to play in the whole of culture, but the role of each is necessarily limited by the distinctive responsibilities and contributions of the other basic aspects. This is true of religion, but it is also true of science. Secular humanism as a form of faith has an important role to play in cultural life, but to claim that it is capable of voiding or replacing all of the historical issues and concerns of religious faith is to take a position that is open to significant debate.

In the third section of the chapter, I call attention to two meanings of the term *science*. The first meaning makes reference to current natural sciences such as physics, chemistry, and biology, or social sciences such as psychology, political science, anthropology, sociology, or economics, while the second meaning focuses on science as representing a *method* of reasoning and establishing truth. When we think about the relations between science and religion, we should be careful to avoid uncritical conflation of these two meanings. The term *science* is sometimes falsely applied exclusively to the first meaning, as if only the disciplines of natural and social sciences employed, or were capable of employing, dependable methods of establishing truth or gaining insight and wisdom. But in fact, modes of reasoning similar to those commonly practiced by the special sciences are also practiced and highly regarded by many proponents of religion, as I shall endeavor to show in this section.

It is a glaring falsehood to claim that only competent scientists make use of methods of sound reasoning and therefore that only their findings are to be respected, while religious people as a whole are guilty of thoughtless fideism and naive credulity, with no responsible basis for their claims. This view turns a blind eye to the history of religions and much of the reasoning of great religious teachers through the centuries and in today's world. The distinction between religion and secularism should not be allowed to rest on a distorting caricature of religion or of any other aspect of culture.

What is this second sense of the term *science*? The philosopher John Dewey is one of its most influential proponents, and we shall investigate the philosophical meaning and central importance he assigns to the concept and method of scientific reasoning in section three. This concept and method understood as Dewey understands them—and rightly, in my view—are applicable within the field of religion as much as it is in other fields of experience and thought. It is therefore wrong to restrict its use or emphasis on its importance only to scientific thinkers.

Religion's Indebtedness to the Sciences

In order to show how deeply religion is dependent on the findings of the sciences, I want to focus in this section on the idea of *decentering*. I focus first on the natural sciences in this regard and then discuss the decentering effects of the social sciences as well. The decentering impacts of these two basic areas of science have produced profound changes in contemporary culture, and these changes have equally profound implications for religion in our time. These impacts have set in motion strikingly different and in many ways much richer and more convincing ways of viewing the world and the role of human beings in the world. In doing so, they have also provided valuable resources for reenvisioning the character and role of religion and its relations to secularism. Far from being by its nature obstinately opposed to developments in the natural and social sciences, much of today's religious thought is in fact deeply in their debt.

The decentering effects of the natural sciences can be seen first in the scientific revolution of the early modern era. The conjoining of mathematical analysis with precise empirical observation and testing in this period had the effect of showing clearly and decisively that our earth is not the center of the universe, but that it orbits the sun. Later development showed just as conclusively that our solar system is a tiny part of the larger Milky Way collection of innumerable stars and planets. In the third decade of the twentieth century it became evident that the Milky Way is a particular galaxy among many others. And we have strong reason to believe today that there are billions of such galaxies in the universe, each with its complements of billions of stars and their own planetary systems. The diameter of the observable universe is thought at present to be a staggering ninety-one billion light years. There is reliable evidence that the universe started expanding early in its evolution and that distant galaxies are moving away from earth *at a much higher rate* than the closer ones.

Thus our relatively little planet earth has been radically decentered in its relation to the incredibly vast, ever-expanding universe as a whole. If we couple this insight with the distinct possibility that the present universe is only one universe that has come into being over infinite, primordial time, and that it will likely be succeeded by an infinite series of new universes to come after it, then the earth's history and all the history of humans and their civilizations on the earth must be seen in a radically new light. We know that our solar system evolved, and we now recount how the present universe evolved in various stages from the supposed Big Bang to the present. So the basically static universe of Aristotle and even of Isaac Newton has given way, under scientific scrutiny, to a dynamic, continually evolving universe as a whole—to say nothing of the particular processes of evolution, terrestrial and biological, that have marked the history of the earth from its origin to the present.

The mention of biological evolution reminds us of how a scientifically informed culture in the West and many other parts of the world has moved in less than two hundred years from the idea that humans, as well as all of the other creatures of earth, were specially created by God, to the current scientific view that all of earth's creatures, including the human ones, have been brought into being through natural evolutionary processes. This idea, and the scientific evidence in its favor, sent a shock wave through a complacent nineteenth-century Christian civilization, as did the new scientific notion that the earth has had a history stretching over millions and even billions of years—meaning that it could not have been literally created in its entirety over a six-day period by divine fiat. The now commonly assumed idea of evolution, as pertaining to the history of the present universe as a whole—and as continuing to operate throughout the vast universe as well as on planet earth—has radically decentered human beings from their long-assumed dominant position on earth to a lesser position of one sort of evolved earthly organism among millions of others, the later ones evolving from the adaptive adventures and misadventures of earlier ones. Moreover, the decentering of earth itself in the context of a massive universe has opened up the strong possibility that there are numerous other life forms—including ones on other planets that are similar to or even superior to humans—throughout the universe.

When these ideas are accompanied by the concept of intricate and necessary ecological interdependency among all of earth's life forms, then humans can no longer be assumed to be somehow outside of nature, set over against it, or fundamentally different from it, but must now be recognized as an integral part of earth's biomass and ecological systems. Biological evolution and intricate ecological interdependency are two fundamental kinds of radical decentering of human beings from their formerly assumed dominant and separate place on earth and even in the universe as whole. We humans can no longer be readily conceived as the crown of nature, as the divinely decreed raison d'être of nature's existence, or as having spiritual souls independent of our bodies that set us apart from all of the rest of nature. It is true that some religious people see these decentering effects of modern science as woeful threats to long established religious beliefs. But these effects also can and need to be recognized as essential ingredients in an inspiring new way of conceiving and living with staunch religious faith and commitment. The universe disclosed by the natural sciences is in many striking respects far more awesome, wondrous, and sublime than the earlier religious one.

Secular celebrations of these scientific developments can be accompanied and have widely been accompanied by willing religious accommodations and adjustments as well. Many religious thinkers of recent times and of the present have sought to come to terms in positive, grateful ways, with these new scientific developments. The scientific decentering of earth, then the solar system, then the Milky Way in the context of hundreds of billions of other galaxies, of life on earth in relation to the distinct possibility of life elsewhere in the universe, and of human life in relation to the myriad other kinds of life on earth at present and in the distant past—all of these developments have opened up exciting, captivating new ways of thinking religiously about the universe and our place as humans within it. Religious faith has always been informed by the cultures of its times, and it continues to be so informed today. A principal force in contemporary culture is the natural sciences, and if religion is to have relevance and credibility in today's world, it needs to be kept in close conversation with these sciences.

One essential effect of such ongoing conversation relates to the concept of God in theistic religions such as Judaism, Christianity, and Islam. The traditional concept of God in these religions has often tended to be anthropomorphic—a concept based to a significant extent on the central place accorded to human beings on earth in these religious traditions. The decentering of humans I am describing has raised new questions and concerns about the anthropomorphic tendency of much earlier thinking about God. Warnings against too literal attribution of human traits to God have not been lacking in theistic religious traditions, but these have still persisted in thinking of God as a distinct person with traits markedly similar to those of human persons but somehow elevated to an infinite degree. The decentering of humans and their coming to be seen as tiny parts of an incredibly ancient and immense universe have encouraged proponents of theistic religions to think anew about the traditional view of God and to try to envision a God of stature and size adequate enough to be the God of the universe as a whole, and not just a God who is concerned almost exclusively with the affairs of planet earth and who focuses predominantly on human beings and their histories and civilizations.

The social sciences, for their part, have posed problems but also presented opportunities for desirable changes and developments of religion in these times. Along with the natural sciences, which they have been motivated by and have sought in many aspects of their research and reasoning to emulate, the social sciences have also had the effect of decentering religion from the dominant cultural roles it played in earlier times. Cultural anthropology, sociology, political science, historiography, economics, and psychology, for example, have become specific types of social science. And these now perform many of the tasks formerly allocated to religious institutions or to institutions guided by sacred scriptures, revered religious authorities, and relatively unquestioned religious convictions. Even when philosophy was called upon to help articulate and defend these convictions, it was almost exclusively *religious* philosophy in the past—a philosophy that took for granted most of the fundamental religious attitudes and beliefs of the time.

What can be considered, at least in some significant ways, as the social sciences of psychology, psychiatry, and medicine are instructive in this regard. The religiously rooted and directed spiritual counseling of an earlier time has now been complemented by, or in many cases supplanted by, widespread psychological counseling of patients in the present. The current discipline of psychiatry that is based in neuroscience as a subset of biology is both a natural and a social science in its own right. But it tends more toward the natural science side. Other types of psychology endeavor to be scientific in their outlooks and methods but generally fall more on the side of social science than of natural science. Modern medicine as a whole can be considered a social science to the extent that it is practiced for the sake of analyzing in a scientific manner the causes and ways of alleviating the effects of human illnesses—especially when these take the form of widespread diseases or plagues—although medicine is very much a natural science in other respects. Medical recommendation of universal vaccinations for the prevention of various kinds of disease have profound social effects, as do medicine's ways of dealing with communities suffering as a whole from some kind of threatening disease. There are also medical warnings to society as a whole of such things as dangerous foods, unhealthy habits, or life-threatening agricultural or industrial practices. Medicine is of course also an animal science, and not just a social science, in the form of veterinary medicine. But animal science has wide-ranging human social effects. Thus psychology, psychiatry, and medicine in general have both natural science aspects and social science ones.

Religious modes of therapy and ways of dealing with mental afflictions, neuroses, or illnesses still continue in such fashions as prayers and rituals for the sick in body or mind, and there were types of primitive medical care that preceded the development of modern scientific medicine in all cultures, sometimes in what were essentially theocracies or societies dominated by theistic religions. But these earlier religious approaches to disease, whether mental or physical, have been radically decentered and diversified by such new kinds of treatment as psychology, psychiatry, and the many kinds of contemporary medicine dependent on the natural sciences.

To say that these social sciences have altered our ways of being in the world and regarding the world would be a colossal understatement. They have shifted our focus throughout the contemporary world from an older culture largely dominated by religion to a new one in which religion has been decentered in favor of numerous new ways of thinking and acting. Who among us would want to go back to an earlier time devoid of the ministrations, assurances, and cures of modern medicine?

Sociology is another kind of social science that has come into prominence in recent times. It uses scientific techniques of description, analysis, and explanation to study social structures, institutions, and practices of various kinds—both in order to understand how they work and to propose ways of refining them. It analyzes the distinctive social roles of various kinds of major societal endeavor and seeks to understand how these roles relate to one another. Political, judicial, educational, financial, communal, family, military, athletic, and religious aspects of society are parts of its purview.

The fact that religious institutions, beliefs, and practices are subjected to extensive sociological investigation implies another kind of decentering of religion. Its teachings are no longer taken for granted as the major source of existential purpose, value, and meaning for individuals, their societies, and their cultures. Instead, religion and its functions in societies are exposed to dispassionate scientific study, with no commitment, one way or the other, to religion's central teachings. Religion is analyzed for its latent social functions and for the roles it plays in culture or society, rather than for the sake of weighing in the balance the truth or falsity, value or disvalue, of its manifest teachings and practices. This approach is a legitimate way of studying religion, but it subordinates its internal teachings and practices to an avowedly more objective, external, and scientific way of thinking. Religion has much to learn from this kind of analysis when it is carefully implemented—a responsible view from without rather than merely the view from within—a way of trying to understand the social effects of religious people's beliefs and of religious institutions as part of the wider society.

In similar fashion, the psychology of religion can subject religious phenomena to careful psychological analysis. Much can be learned in this way about religious factors in mental illness, for example, with a resulting ability to help patients to recognize and deal with these factors in their afflictions. Political scientists, to cite another social science, are naturally interested in the attitudes and influences of religious persons and groups to the extent that these attitudes and influences affect political practices and outcomes. Religion not only affects society, but it is affected in countless ways by nonreligious cultural and societal influences, and it is important for both religious and nonreligious people to understand what these are and how they work.

However, religion is not reducible to or replaceable by the descriptive, explanatory, ameliorative, or hortatory functions of the natural or social sciences. To claim that all that is of lasting value in religion can somehow be *exhaustively* analyzed and substituted for by the physical and natural sciences—a claim made by more than a few secular thinkers—is to extend the scope of these disciplines beyond their proper boundaries. It is also to betray, more often than not, a superficial understanding of the full range of religious thought and experience through the ages and is to overlook today the perennial role of distinctively religious questions, searches, and commitments as a fundamental part of the human condition—a role that cannot be adequately comprehended or sufficiently encompassed by the natural or social sciences or by secular thinkers who reject all religion out of hand and deny in the name of science religion's lasting importance.

The role of religion in society is sometimes deleterious or destructive, as when religious people and religious institutions give unquestioning obedience to religious teachers in political and other social affairs, or when they uncritically incite or support havoc-wreaking conflicts and wars on this basis. But the role of secular thinkers can be no less damaging when they grant—as they sometimes do—equally uncritical authority to secular-minded teachers and leaders. Firsthand critical analysis is desperately needed in both areas of thought, not just in the religious one. It is also needed when it comes to the claims of scientists, especially when these claims encroach on the competencies and concerns of other basic areas of thought.

Limitations of the Sciences

The approaches, techniques, and practices of the natural and social sciences have great and undeniable importance in the cultures of our time, but it is a mistake to think of their purview as either presently or potentially all-comprehending or all-encompassing, as I now intend to show. Science is a particular part of culture. The scientific fields are no more entitled to dominate the whole of culture with claims to absolute authority over all thought and action than were Roman Catholic or Muslim religions in medieval times or certain Protestant religious groups in more recent times. The alleged hegemony of the sciences over other aspects of culture, whether religious, moral, political, aesthetic, or philosophical, should be strongly resisted. Each of the important aspects of culture limits the ranges of the other aspects, and such limitation is true of science in all of its guises, with frank acknowledgment of its indispensable contributions, and with due respect for its undeniably important roles in present society. Secularists as well as religionists should keep these crucial observations about the natural and social sciences in mind.

The natural and social sciences are limited by their relations to other basic aspects of human culture, aspects that they are neither entitled nor competent to encompass or dominate. They are also limited in at least three other ways. First, when the approaches of science are behavioral or operational in their appeals to shared sensate experiences, or when they rely only on personal reports given to researchers, they do partial but cannot do full justice to the internal, firsthand, phenomenological areas of deeply searching human feeling, aspiring, and experiencing, and the irreplaceable importance of these personal experiences to human beings. It is one thing for a psychologist or social scientist to register and reflect on someone's description or identification of such experience; it is another to *have* the experiences and to ponder their import with *firsthand* awareness.

The desperate search and crying need for existential meaning, purpose, and value that has characterized humankind from the remote past to the present cannot be adequately addressed or resolved by the secondhand approaches of the sciences, especially when *only* the assertions and conclusions of these sciences are claimed to have the possibility of being responsibly evaluated for their truth and reliability. Outcomes of scientific reporting, generalizing, and appraising should be taken carefully into account—to the extent that they are relevant—by firsthand reflection and judging. But they cannot substitute for the firsthand experiences. I'll have more to say about this crucial point later in the chapter.

Second, the sciences are typically descriptive and explanatory and in consequence not able to assess with full competency or adequacy the valuative dimensions of art, morality, or religion, which have to do primarily with particular ways of seeking *justification* for these values—not just describing them, explaining in a causal way why people or institutions hold to them, or simply recounting ways in which they may be claimed to be justified. It is one thing to poll people for their commitments in the quest for some kind of general societal analysis of these commitments. It is another to attempt to justify or criticize these commitments in an appropriate manner. If I tell a pollster what my belief concerning a particular valuative issue is, and the transcription of my belief becomes part of a data set to be used in a research project, this procedure is different from inquiring into whether or not the valuative commitment itself is justified. Causes for my having the commitment can be inquired into scientifically, but justification of it as a personal value or conviction lies to a significant extent outside the province of the physical or social sciences. It is one thing to pay careful attention to these sciences in arriving at my valuative commitments. This is often important and necessary. It is another to think that the commitments should be, or can always be arrived at *solely* on the basis of these sciences.

The logic of explanation is different from the logic of justification. To explain why I have a certain set of religious beliefs, in the causal sense of "why," is not the same thing as my being able to give relevant reasons for my commitment to them. To believe in something because my parents or friends believe in it does not amount to a justification of the belief. The justificatory reasons for valuative commitments will include ultimate appeals to personal modes of ever-developing experience and awareness that cannot be fully described or made patent or plausible to someone else, but that have become deeply convincing to me. Adequate understanding of the reasons—to say nothing of their convictional power—may require persisting disciplines of meditative, introspective thought that are different from the disciplines of a particular science.

I cannot jump from the outside and without sufficient and relevant preparation into the depths of religious experience and into reasons for conviction and belief that draw profoundly on religious experience, for example, any more than I can jump into the role of an art critic. Both require skills of inquiry, perception, and adjudication that, in the final analysis, are deeply personal. And the personal often cannot be translated into the public arena without significant loss. Something similar to this deeply personal acumen and awareness is required in the training of scientists as well. They must learn how to detect promising leads for scientific explanation and how to follow them up successfully—in other words, how to master the art of scientific investigation and the enduring motivations for its pursuit that cannot simply be described, taught, or contained in a manual or set of rules. The receptivity and capability of being taught must already be present and await development. Such attitudes and aptitudes are the preconditions of science, not just its outcomes. They are brought to it, and not derived from it.

And third, science is far from being a bastion of irrefutable truths even within its selective domain of culture. There is often a plurality of contending views within the sciences, especially on cutting-edge issues of continuing inquiry and development in the physical sciences such as the puzzling interactions between the quantum world and the macro world, the true natures and relations of space and time, the choice between string theory or loop quantum gravity, the natures of dark energy and dark matter, or the problem of how to reconcile certain central aspects of current quantum theory with Einstein's general theory of relativity.

There are similar if not even more unresolved theoretical divisions within the social sciences. There is Freudian psychology, behavioral psychology, and cognitive psychology, for example. And there is Keynesian economics and Friedmanian (or Hayekian) economics. So neither the natural nor the social sciences should be regarded as irrefutable monuments of truth. Many physical and social scientific claims are limited by other scientific claims that are currently taking issue with them—and some of these claims are foundational rather than superficial.

Moreover, long-established and even the most basic scientific claims to truth are sometimes overthrown by later scientific developments. None of us—scientist or nonscientist—can know with certainty what modifications to or abandonments of current major or minor scientific theories might be brought about in the future, and brought about in ways we cannot presently even imagine. The natural as well as the social sciences have limits within themselves and not just beyond themselves. A principal internal limit for all of them, as I also indicated earlier in this chapter, is the unknowability of the future.

Two Conceptions of Science

I made reference earlier in this chapter to two different meanings of science or of scientific reasoning. The first one is restricted to the *particular natural sciences* such as physics, chemistry, or biology and to subsets of these fields such quantum physics, organic chemistry, or cell biology, and can include the social sciences—according to this view—only to the extent that the latter are firmly rooted in, strictly guided by, and fundamentally like the physical sciences, with a putatively purely external, objective, or publicly verifiable approach to all phenomena, whether physical, mental, social, political, and so forth. The second meaning makes reference to a *specific method* for arriving at truth and value, a method that can be applied and put to use in all domains of thought and aspiration, not just within the special physical and social sciences.

One type of secularism is the idea that the particular physical and social sciences encompass, at least in principle, all of reality, including both its factual and its valuative aspects, and that we should endeavor to bring everything of importance in the universe under the umbrella of one or more of these sciences. In other words, if we cannot treat a problem as one that falls under the competency of the particular sciences, and especially the physical ones, then it is a pseudoproblem.

This outlook is a kind of secularism because, among other things, it rejects religion on the ground that its characteristic concerns either do not fit into those of science as so described or that they can only be adequately addressed when converted into scientific concerns and addressed by one or more of the special sciences. A name for this all-encompassing, all-assimilating view of the particular sciences is *scientism*, which Alfred I. Tauber, philosopher and bioethicist at Boston University, defines as "the fundamental notion that reality is consonant with, if not superimposable on, the picture of reality that science offers" (2009: 13). And by *science*, he means here the particular physical and social sciences. Tauber rightly rejects scientism in favor of a much more capacious view of reality that takes fully into account the contributions of the humanistic disciplines, such as philosophy, religious studies, history, and art, to our understanding of the many-faceted world and the place of humans in the world.

For Tauber, there is even an important sense in which the physical sciences themselves need to be brought into searching sociological perspective in order for their historical developments, influences, and natures to be properly understood. In other words, the physical sciences are situated within and dependent on other perspectives, and do not simply include all of them as their alleged ultimate container. One way to see this point is to reflect on the fact that all of the sciences, whether physical or social, rest on a bed of assumed values that must continue to be brought to the test of ongoing experience as proofs of their importance and plausibility. These assumed values include curiosity, persistence, patience, honesty, accuracy, collegiality, openness to opposing points of view, and willingness to accept the risks of making mistakes in order to learn from them. The famous fact-value dichotomy founders on the realization that assumed values such as these are essential to the pursuit of scientific truth in all domains of thought and experience. None of the sciences could exist or have credibility without these assumed values.

The particular physical and social sciences are of great importance for Tauber, as they are for me, but they are not *all-important* for either of us. They encompass crucial areas of thought and experience but are far from encompassing all of the important areas. They make decisive contributions to our knowledge and awareness but do not constitute the only reliable kinds of knowledge and awareness. More particularly, and this is the point of special relevance to the themes of this book, an alleged but implausible reduction of everything to the special physical or social sciences cannot count as a convincing basis on which to opt for secular faith and wholesale rejection of religious faith. So much, then, for the first idea that the term *science* refers exclusively to the particular physical and social sciences and that, in doing so, it raises the issue of the ranges and competencies of these sciences.

The second main connotation of the term *science* is that of a method, habit, or mode of reasoning that is not restricted to the particular physical and social sciences but can and should be put to prominent use in *all* areas of thought. This kind of reasoning often goes by the name of science or more accurately *scientific method*, and it is illustrated by what typically goes on in the reasoning of the natural sciences. However, the original Latin meaning of *scientia* is simply "knowledge," and this second meaning is not restricted to any particular discipline or search for knowledge but is intended to apply, whenever proper or important, to all fields.

Among thinkers who have made important contributions to our understanding of what science regarded as a method of inquiry is all about and how it is capable of contributing to every important area of thought is the American philosopher John Dewey. In what follows, I summarize his conception of science as the application of scientific method to every aspect of the experienced world—a conception that is developed in his book *The Quest for Certainty*, and especially in the last two chapters of this magisterial work.

What is this so-called scientific method of inquiry or way of establishing and making perspicuous and reliable crucial meanings, truths, and values? For Dewey, it requires abandonment of the notion that truths or values already exist in some realm antecedent to their investigation and discovery, that is, that they somehow float free of their critical involvements in our experiences of the world. Truths and values are probabilistic at best and do not admit of any kind of inviolable or absolute certainty. Their initial forms are *ideals* posited as *possibilities* of attainment, not already existent realities that just await our intellectual recognition and application. As ideals, they function as empirical *hypotheses* that need to be put to the test of relevant kinds of experience.

Each hypothesis says in effect, "If this conjecture is true or valuable, then it will have certain specifically describable consequences or effects in ongoing experience. Subject it to relevant empirical tests to see if this is indeed the case." Only when the putative truth or value, or more properly the hypothesis that formulates or expresses a claim to it, is put to the test of experience, does it become an established truth or value for a particular kind of inquiry—whether that be scientific, philosophical, artistic, moral, or religious. Pure thought can imagine or propose such hypotheses, but it cannot confirm them. Only experience can do that. Various types of mathematics would also fit into this model of speculative ideals functioning as hypotheses for empirical testing.[1]

For Dewey, all dependable truths and values are outcomes of consciously directed empirical inquiry; they have no status as realities—only as possibilities—prior to such inquiry. Their test is not some kind of elegant, seductive appeal to the rational mind detached from experience but is solely the consequences they are predicted to have in relevant types of experience or practice.

The scientific method as Dewey understands it, then, has three aspects: formulation of an explicit hypothesis about some kind of tentative truth or value; discerning the consequences the hypothesis can be expected to have in experience; and seeing if, when put into practice, it turns out to have these empirical consequences. In this manner and only in this manner, can truths and values be established and meaningfully incorporated into our visions of the world and ways of living in the world. They can be said to exist as realities only to the extent that they continue to guide and inform experience in each of the areas where they are being put constantly to the test. This test is pragmatic and ongoing. To the extent that it is successful and continues to be so, it can give us reliable knowledge of truth and value in all the domains of thought, experience, and aspiration.

But all claims to truth and value are fallible. There is no such thing as absolute insurance against error. And all of the stopping points of inquiry are temporary because they may be overruled by some presently unimagined or unexpected new ways of thinking or experiencing. The face of scientific method so described is therefore always toward the future, not merely to the past. Past ideas, no matter how habitual and deep-rooted they may have become in the present, are to be seen as hypotheses subject to continual testing. This is as true in the particular physical and social scientific disciplines as it is in in all other areas of thought, including the area of religion. Columbia University professor in the biological sciences Stuart Firestein speaks knowledgably when he says, "In science, there are invariably loose ends and little blind allies. While you may think you have everything cleared up, there is always something new and unexpected. But there is value in uncertainty. It shouldn't create anxiety. It's an opportunity" (Borel 2019: 86). Nima Arkani-Hamed, a theoretical physicist at the Institute for Advanced Study in Princeton, New Jersey, makes essentially the same point when he observes, "At any moment in history, we can understand some aspects of the world but not everything. When a revolutionary change brings in more of the larger picture, we have to reconfigure what we knew. The old things are still part of the truth but have to be spun around and put back into the larger picture in a new way" (Borel 2019: 91).

Why, I now ask, should it be any different for religious outlooks and convictions? Here too we need to face toward the future rather than being fixated on the beliefs of the past. Here too something closely akin to Dewey's conception of scientific method is required. The past provides vitally useful resources and suggested hypotheses for continual testing, revising, applying, and in some cases abandoning older beliefs in light of new experiences, and with constant awareness of the possibility of even more novel ways of thinking and experiencing that may lie over the horizon of an unknown and presently unknowable future.

The religious experiences to which I make reference here are, more often than not, profoundly personal, first-handed, and existential in their character. Only the individual, in the final analysis, can contemplate and decide on the truths and values of personal religious matters or matters relating to the fundamental meanings, values, and purposes of each person's life. No one else can arrive at an individual person's deeply felt religious convictions or make binding religious or other kinds of existential decisions on the individual person's behalf.

As Alfred North Whitehead sagely observes of religion, it "is the art and theory of the internal life of man, so far as it depends on the man himself. . . ." Continuing in this vein, he writes,

> This doctrine is the direct negation of the theory that religion is primarily a social fact. Social facts are of great importance to religion, because there is no such thing as an absolutely independent existence. You cannot abstract society from man; most psychology is herd-psychology. But all collective emotions leave untouched the awful ultimate fact, which is the human being, consciously alone with itself, for its own sake.

He concludes that "religion is what the individual does with his own solitariness" and that "if you are never solitary, you are never religious" (1926: 16–17).

An individual can report to others on the individual's solitary religious musings and decisions and act out their implications in the presence of others, thus projecting them into the public realm. But only the individual can experience and respond to these factors of self-awareness personally and in the context of firsthand reflection, memory, anticipation, and awareness. These factors are existential and cannot be made external without loss of their central existential character. They are thus beyond reach of the final adjudication or appraisal of the particular sciences. But most importantly, these experiences can function as the test of hypotheses relating to the deepest areas of life, in the manner of which Dewey speaks, a manner he describes as *scientific* or even, more simply and comprehensively, as *science*, in the broad senses of these two terms.

Secularists who deny the availability or appropriateness of this scientific way of thinking, reacting, and behaving to religious traditions, institutions, and persons—and who oppose and take issue with religion primarily if not solely on the ground of its failure to be scientific or responsive to scientific ways of thinking, fail to take notice of the fact that their assumption about the nature of religion does not do justice to the second meaning of the term *science* or to all types of religious faith. These types range from the most avowedly primitivist or backward-looking perspectives dedicated to replicating as far as possible in the present the remote religious past and to literalistic understandings of sacred texts as though they transcend and envelope all time, to the most progressive-minded religious explorations of every aspect of present cultural experience for the sake of appropriating and revising past texts, traditions, and beliefs in ways judged to be religiously relevant to the present and the future. Religion is no simple or easily described feature of history, culture, or society. It has many forms and should not be restricted to one conception or one form. In similar fashion, secularism has many forms, and I am calling attention to a glaringly implausible form of it in this paragraph.

But is it not the case that all religious people insist on the *certainty* or *undeniability* of their central religious teachings and beliefs? They do seek assurance or confidence that can count as a kind of *existential* certainty or certainty of conviction. But this is not the same thing as insisting on the *epistemic* certainty of any particular set of beliefs. The beliefs are unlikely in any event to capture the deep-lying lived certainty or firm confidence of conviction that marks strong religious faith. Moreover, the profound sense of mystery that infuses authentic religious faith militates against claims to the absolute epistemic certainty of any collection of religious beliefs. Not only is probability enough for the status of these beliefs from a religious perspective, but it is an essential characteristic of them.

I can offer two striking examples of how revered religious teachings can function as hypotheses, in Dewey's sense of the term, which must be put continually to the test of ongoing personal experience in order to ascertain their meaning, value, and truth. The first example is from the Pāli Texts of Theravada Buddhism. A Buddhist disciple, Kālāmas, questions his teacher on behalf of his fellow disciples with the following question: "For us, venerable sir, there is doubt as to which of these good ascetics speak truth and which speak falsehood." The teacher answers:

> It is fitting for you to be perplexed, O Kālāmas; it is fitting for you to be in doubt. Do not go by oral tradition, by lineage of teaching, by a collection of texts, by logic, by inferential reasoning, by reasoning cogitation, by the acceptance of a view after pondering it, by the seeming competence of a speaker, or because you think, "the ascetic is our teacher." But when you know *for yourselves*, "These things are unwholesome; these things are blamable; these things are censured by the wise; these things, if undertaken and practiced, lead to harm and suffering," then you should abandon them. (Bodhi 2005: 89; my italics)

The teacher does not censure the student for having doubts about religious teachings, traditions, and the like. He invites him to entertain these matters as being hypothetical claims to truth and value that can only be confirmed or repudiated when put to the test of the student's firsthand experience. The confirmation or repudiation cannot be provided by any presumed authorities, no matter how venerable or esteemed these may be. It cannot be given by abstract logical or inferential reasoning. The test must be experiential: a matter of taking seriously various possible candidates for truth and value and then submitting these candidates to the test of one's own ongoing personal experience. The Buddha discovered his teachings through long and arduous searching and experiencing; these teachings must be put to the test and rediscovered at firsthand by each and every student of Buddhism.

This way of thinking is pretty close to Dewey's conviction that ideals of truth and value are just that—ideal possibilities, not antecedent or already real truths and values—and that these ideals become existentially important and meaningful for seekers in all domains, including the domain of religion, only when the seekers are honest enough and earnest enough to raise deep questions about them and to put the ideals continuously to the test of the relevant kinds of experience.

Theravada Buddhism does not advocate blind credulity or thoughtless submission to authority; it requires that all putative authorities be treated as presenting hypotheses whose final tests must experiential. Can this claim to religious truth or value be lived, appropriated into the depths of my life, giving inspiration, direction, and support to the whole of my life? Can I continue to put it to the test in my daily experience, deepening my understanding and appropriation of it as my experience develops and unfolds? I can live in community with others who are embarked on a similar religious path, and I can receive valuable instruction and guidance from members of the community. But no one of them can provide the conviction that I can gain only by ongoing personal testing of the possible truths and values proclaimed by great religious teachers, texts, and traditions.

A conception of religious faith similar to the Buddhist one is presented by Episcopal priest and college teacher of world religions Barbara Brown Taylor when she notes how often the Jesus of the Gospels responded to people who raised questions with him by asking thought-provoking questions of them in return. She writes,

> Jesus seems to know more about the way of transformation than many of his followers do. If someone wants to know more about God, he implies, it will involve more than believing someone else's answers. It will involve thinking deeply about the questions you are asking and why. Then it will involve acting on the answers you come up with in order to discover what is true. (2019: 57)

Something similar to this process takes place when religious seekers ponder Zen koans or other kinds of enigmatic stories, parables, symbols, myths, or rituals in order to discover for themselves what possible religious truths and values can be found there to be incorporated into their lives.

The experiences to which I make reference here are, more often than not, profoundly personal, first-handed, phenomenological, and existential in their character. Only the individual, in the final analysis, can contemplate and decide on the truths and values of personal religious matters. No one else can arrive at an individual person's religious convictions or make religious decisions on the individual person's behalf.

An individual can *report on* solitary religious musings and decisions and *act out* their implications, thus putting them into the public realm, but only the individual can *experience* these factors of self-awareness at firsthand. I cannot directly access your personal field of awareness, and you cannot access mine. Such personal musings and decisions are existential and cannot be made external without loss of their central existential character. They are thus finally beyond the reach of external adjudication or appraisal. Nevertheless, these deeply personal experiences can function as one kind of experiential test of hypotheses of which Dewey speaks. Intensely personal or existential religious experiences can be instructed and informed by the reported religious experiences of others. They can be shared with, and in that way possibly contribute to, the religious experience and awareness of others. And there is the important test of the truth of a person's religious convictions by the observable qualities, values, and contributions of that person's life. In these three ways, proponents of religious conviction and belief can interact with the experiences of others and bring their personal experiences into the public domain for critical discussion and appraisal.

In the final analysis, religious beliefs are feeble pointers to the depths of mystery to which great religious systems allude and to the profoundly felt but finally indescribable existential convictions of religious persons, communities, or traditions they reflect. But even these central existential convictions are susceptible to possible change over time, meaning that the assurance they may once have had in the lives of particular persons or communities is no longer present. They may have given way to another kind of religious faith, or religious faith itself may have given way to some form of secular faith. In similar fashion, there are possible conversions from secular to religious forms of faith. There is no escape from the fallibilities of belief or even from the susceptibilities to change of deeply implanted stances of faith over a lifetime.[2]

Dewey refers to a naturalistic kind of religious faith that also falls under his pragmatic epistemology and conception of scientific method as applying to all responsible domains of thought when he writes, "Religious faith which attaches itself to the possibilities of nature and associated living would, with its devotion to the ideal, manifest piety toward the actual." A bit further on in the same passage, he insists that "nature, including humanity, with all its defects and imperfections, may evoke heartfelt piety as the source of ideals, of possibilities, of aspiration in their behalf, and as the eventual abode of all attained goods and excellencies" (1960: 306). Here there is reference to a type of religious faith that makes no mention of anything beyond the natural—that is, to nothing supernatural—but finds profound religious meaning and assurance in the unfathomable wonders, challenges, and mysteries of nature. The focus of this kind of "piety toward the actual," as Dewey aptly terms it, is entirely on nature as we experience it and contemplate it here-and-now, not on some imagined radically different, faraway, purely spiritual world.

Such piety can join secularism in rejecting the need for anything supernatural, but it finds in the awesome depths and mysteries of nature, when properly contemplated and experienced, all that it is needed for richly sustaining religious life. For natural piety, nature is an inexhaustible store of potential truths and values to be brought to the tests of experience and to grow in probable but constantly confirming truth and value to the extent that they continue to meet these necessary tests. Theravada Buddhism, a prominent teaching method of the Jesus of the Gospels, and religious naturalism are therefore three examples of religious commitment and outlook on the world that lie within the scope of Dewey's analysis. I submit that, at their best, other religious traditions do as well.

Conclusion

The contention of a certain kind of secularism is that we can no longer regard any type of religion as plausible because we live in a scientific age and must subject all beliefs and values to the test of scientific ways of thinking. The secularist argument in this case is that religious faith does not depend on and could not pass such tests; therefore we should abandon it. The point is said to apply with special force to an alleged appeal by all religions to supernatural realms, presences, persons, or powers that are claimed to lie beyond the reach of scientific investigation.

I take strong issue in the present chapter with this kind of secularist argument when it is applied to all forms of religious faith, just as I took issue in the two previous chapters with a kind of secularist assumption—

acknowledged or implicit—that all religions dream of some kind of timeless or everlasting existence for human beings, or that all religions lay claim to and depend finally on far-fetched claims to infallible truths. No sharp line between secular and religious forms of faith can be drawn, I argue, on any or all of these three bases.

I argue in this chapter that, far from being opposed to science, religion has much to learn from science and should willingly and gratefully modify, adjust, or expand its teachings in light of what it learns. Many contemporary forms of religion give evidence of having done so and continuing to do so. I also argue against the hegemonic picture of the particular sciences as dominating and controlling all other areas of thought as though these latter, when properly understood, can have legitimacy only to the extent that they can be brought under the umbrella of the specific disciplines of the natural or social sciences.

I hold that *science*, when this term is thought to refer exclusively to the particular sciences, is only one dimension of culture among others, and that the others cannot be absorbed without residue into one or more of these sciences. Religion is a prominent one of these different cultural dimensions, and its irreducibility into *science*, as the latter term is taken to mean in the use under discussion here, is no sufficient reason to reject its continuing relevance and meaning in the modern world. This would be embarrassingly similar to a rightly condemned attempt to reduce all that is of importance in the special sciences to the cultural domain of religion.

I call attention in this chapter to two significantly different meanings of the term *science* that need to be explicitly distinguished. The first meaning refers to the natural and social sciences, and especially to the natural sciences of physics, chemistry, and biology. As already indicated, I reject the claim that everything of value in religion can either be swallowed up into one or more of these sciences or must be rejected when this type of reduction proves to be unfeasible. The second meaning of *science* makes reference to a method of reasoning that can be broadly characterized as science, given the fact that it is most tellingly exemplified in the reasonings of the special sciences. Religion is quite capable of putting this method of reasoning into regular use, I argue, and to claim that no religion does so or can do so is plainly fallacious.

I defend this case by drawing on the way in which philosopher John Dewey characterizes scientific thought—that is, carefully directed empirical and pragmatic reasoning—seeing it as identical with the most dependable, respectable, cogent reasoning in all areas of thought, including the area of religion. It is possible in this manner to view religion as amenable to scientific modes of reasoning but also as not reducible to any of the natural or social sciences, given religion's distinctive areas of inquiry, thought, and concern as important aspects of human history and present culture.

Science is a threat to religion only when the first sense of science is held in mind, namely, that what is of religious significance can either be handled more competently by the special sciences or must be rejected to the extent that it cannot be so handled. But science is a friend to religion in the second sense because it takes fully into account the tentativeness of religious claims and convictions, along with all other kinds of claim and conviction, and subjects the former to ongoing treatments of them as hypotheses subject to modification, amplification, or possible abandonment, depending on how well they can withstand the test of the relevant kinds of anticipated or predicted experiences in an ever-changing cultural and personal world.

The interests and concerns of religion are different in essential ways from those of the special sciences, but the investigatory means for addressing and adjudicating these interests and concerns can be made quite similar and with inestimable religious benefit. This is the larger and more applicable sense of the term *science* to the ongoing analysis, reappropriation, and revision of contemporary religion's distinctive claims to truth and value. There is no more warrant for a secularist rejection of all forms of religious faith in this chapter's third main line of argument than there is in the two supposed bases for such outright rejection discussed in the previous two chapters of this book. So once again, the distinction between religion and secularism cannot be easily made.

Chapter Four

Ambiguities of Nature

> A struggle for existence inevitably follows from the high rate at which all organic beings tend to increase. Every being, which during its natural lifetime produces several eggs or seeds, must suffer destruction during some season or occasional year, otherwise, on the principle of geometrical increase, its numbers would quickly become so inordinately great that no country could support the product. Hence, as more individuals are produced than can possibly survive, there must in every case be a struggle for existence, either one individual with another of the same species, or with the individuals of distinct species, or with the physical conditions of life.
>
> —Charles Darwin (n.d.: 53)

The idea that all religious people by their very nature as religious seek in a number of different ways to escape from nature, whereas secular people readily affirm the great importance and value of nature, and of the place of humans in nature, is a fourth possible way of drawing a fundamental distinction between religion and nonreligion, or the sacred and the secular. But like the other three ways of making this distinction discussed in the previous chapters, this way fails to take into account the many different types of religions and varieties of religious faith. It is true that some religions are emphatically world-denying, but it is also true that some are ardently world-affirming. The former often base their stance of world-denial on the palpable and ever-threatening ambiguities of nature. They dream of a perfect heaven or of a flawless new earth.

Nature is presently, on the one hand, a haven of beauty, support, enjoyment, challenge, and repose. The life it grants to creatures such as we humans are can be enthusiastically welcomed and cherished, not lamentably dismissed and scorned. This is the nature of age-long celebratory story, poetry, painting, and song. But on the other hand, nature is suffused with ominous dangers. Its laws enable life but also threaten its particular forms in innumerable ways. There is the predation and precariousness of earthly life to which Charles Darwin calls attention in the epigraph of this chapter—the dark side of nature that is evident in biological evolution with its vast extinctions of the past and in the ceaseless struggles for survival by all creatures in the earth's ecological systems. Countless new species of life have come into existence by evolution, and countless older ones have perished and vanished forever from the earth as the result of those same evolutionary processes. The creatures of present ecosystems must constantly kill to eat, and they must be killed in order that other creatures can survive. The struggle for survival is harsh and endless. Nature is manifestly pro-life here on earth, but in order to be so, it is also relentlessly pro-death.

Then there are the awesome forces and laws of nature that generally sustain life on earth, at least for extended periods of time, but that also subject it to ever-present and sometimes horrendous accidents, diseases, earthquakes, volcanic eruptions, wildfires, floods, droughts, and storms. Nature is a volatile mixture of creation and destruction, wildly ambiguous in copious benefits conjoined with ever-present hazards. Nature sustains even as it destroys. Its laws are helpful or hurtful, depending on context and circumstance. We humans can never be entirely sure which tendency will come to the fore at any given time. We must somehow find the courage to live in the face of gnawing uncertainty about what the distant or even the proximal future will bring for us and for those we love.

Our bodies are fragile, always susceptible to calamity, accident, and disease, or to dire injury at the hands of others. There is no escape in this world from the sudden or gradual unsheathing of talons of time that will eventually destroy much if not most of all that we hold dear. Our lives are inescapably precarious, and the earth is a hauntingly dangerous place. If we add to these considerations the hazards and hurts that humans inflict on one another by wars, unjust institutions, vengeful acts, jealousies, prejudices, struggles over power and resources, callous disregard for the well-being of one another, and the like, then life on the earth looks even more hopelessly fraught with unnerving ambiguities. The present humanly induced climate crisis and increasingly widespread endangerments of biological species, to a large extent due to lack of appropriate human concern for the well-being of these species and their habitats, augments from another direction the ambiguities and dangers of nature.

In light of all of this—or more properly in the menacing *shadow* of all of this—it comes as no surprise that some people are filled with all-consuming dread and repugnance toward nature and earthly life. They may respond to the ambiguities of nature and the destructive tendencies of human nature with unquenchable feelings of despair, succumbing to nihilism. Or they may seek relief from these threatening ambiguities in otherworldly forms of religion with visions of a future life in a wholly different, allegedly perfect world. Unable or unwilling to come to terms with life in an ambiguous world, they may desperately seek refuge in a radically unambiguous one.

But not all religions have this character, and it is notable that nihilism or rejection of the possibility of meaningful life in a radically ambiguous world is a secular phenomenon of our own and earlier times, not just a religious one. So such rejection is not solely the trait of some religious outlooks. It cuts across the divide between religion and secularity. Despite what some secularists may be inclined to think, it is not the case that all religions or types of religious faith fit the pattern of deploring this world and clinging desperately to the hope of entering into a radically different one. There are world-affirming and world-denying kinds of religion, just as there are world-affirming and world-denying kinds of secularity.

I shall show this to be the case in the present chapter by discussing three aspects of the troubling ambiguities of life in this world: inanimate nature, nonhuman animate nature, and the human side of nature. In these sections, I want to demonstrate that these ambiguities are not only necessary and inevitable in most cases, but that, together with their possibly preventable presence in other cases, they manifest the welcome and cherishable character of nature in its nonhuman and human aspects here on earth. In a fourth section, I discuss three examples of religious outlooks that are resolutely naturalistic and this-worldly in their character, meaning that they strongly reverence and approve the inanimate, nonhuman animate, and human sides of nature, with all of their inherent threats and ambiguities.

Staunch and credible religious faith can therefore acknowledge and affirm a positive, this-worldly point of view, and it can do so without sentimentality or delusion. It can enable us to feel at home in this world with full and grateful recognition of its necessary ambiguities—whether nonhuman or human in their origins—and not to pine for transport into some imagined, allegedly perfect mode of existence believed to be forever safeguarded against all unsettling threat, uncertainty, and ambiguity. In this chapter, therefore, I criticize and reject a fourth way of making a sharp distinction between religious and secular forms of faith, in addition to the other three ways discussed consecutively in the previous three chapters.

Inanimate Nature

A nature of laws is a redundancy. It is in the nature of nature to have laws. Without the regularities and predictabilities ensured by natural laws, there would be chaos, not cosmos. We humans could not plan in dependable ways for the future. We could not exercise meaningful freedom in a chaotic world. We would intend one thing but some other thing would be just as likely to happen. No creature could survive in a world without laws that give reliable structure and order to the world. In fact, there would be no creatures, including human creatures, because natural laws are crucial to the intricate structures and functionings of all bodily organisms, as well as to the evolutionary origins and continuing survivals of all organic species, including the human one. Natural laws can sometimes harm us, and this fact makes for their undeniable and unavoidable ambiguity, but they are much more of a blessing than a curse overall.

A world in which anything can happen at any time because of the absence of laws would be fraught with unbelievable terror at any moment. It would be a living hell, perched always on the brink of unforeseeable disaster. But more fundamentally, it could not even qualify as a world. Instead, there would be nothing more than a constantly shifting kaleidoscope of unrestricted, uncontrolled, uncontrollable events, each one following gratuitously and unpredictably from the other. But there would be neither observers nor victims of such a catastrophic "world." Without dependable laws and regularities nothing could exist for more than a fleeting moment.

The laws of nature do not have to be eternal to qualify as laws. It is possible for older laws to give away to new ones over vast periods of time. But new laws do not arise in a vacuum. They are transformations of older laws made possible by the context and order of those older laws. Antecedent order is requisite for the creation of new order. Without order, there would be no time, because the flow of time is itself a kind of order. Everywhere we look in nature, within ourselves, or in our experiences as natural beings, there is law-like order. We are entitled to take it for granted because it is inevitable.

Is it desirable that there be such a thing as the natural world in which we live day-by-day? If so, then by clear implication it is desirable that there be such a thing as natural laws. The fact that these laws pertain to the whole of nature means that they do not just pertain to us humans in all circumstances or that they will always ensure our personal safety and well-being or that of others close to us. We will sometimes run afoul of the laws of nature, whether deliberately or accidentally, and we or those we love will suffer accordingly. This kind of ambiguity or immanent possibility of help or hurt is in the very nature of things unavoidable.

The gravity that holds us securely onto the surface of a cliff can also maim or kill us if we stumble off the cliff. The fire that cooks our food and warms us in the winter can also, in other circumstances, do us grievous harm. The breeze that cools us in the summer can also take the form of a hurricane that blows off the roof of our house or fells a tree that crushes a part of it, or even one or more of its unwary occupants. The water we drink can also drown us. Natural laws are Janus-like, facing in the two directions of possible support or possible harm. The statistics favor more the support than the harm, but the harm is an ever-present possibility.

Such facts would be unavoidable in any conceivable world, including some kind of heavenly world. The only possible alternative to them would be a world in which a deity or collections of deities constantly intervenes to ensure that no one in the world would ever be harmed. But even this implausible scenario would require that there be a deity or deities with the order of a constantly watchful and helpful nature, and a world in which the effects of its or their decisions can be reliably predicted and successfully implemented. Moreover, there would have to be a different world for each and every sentient being in such a world, since what may be helpful for one being might turn out to be hurtful for another. In other words, in such a world there could be no such things as conflicts of goods, or situations in which, in order to achieve a particular good, another possible good has to be sacrificed.

Does this imagined world of ubiquitous special providences begin to look like a chaos rather than like a world? If so, the point is well taken. Ambiguity and pervasive order go necessarily together. To wish for a world in which this is not the case is to wish for something that has no clear meaning—a world that is not truly a world. It is hard to believe in or hope for something that has no intelligible meaning, because there would be no clarity about what is being wished for. In any case, religion does not have to be tied inextricably to such a hope, and secular-minded people are entirely right to subject it to criticism.

But perhaps in a purely spiritual world, these considerations would not apply. Or perhaps God is not constrained by such considerations. Our ideas about what it takes to have a conceivable world may differ radically from God's, or a realm of being may exist that is far beyond the reach of our thinking and imagining. These are possibilities that can be said by some to override the conceptual impossibilities of humans, which is another way of assigning a fundamental role to unquestioning assent or blind faith.

But there is a crucial distinction between blind faith and reasonable faith, and my discussions in this book are focused on what can count as reasonable beliefs and affirmations of religious faith. From the standpoint of reasonable faith, a supposed world without regular, pervasive, predictable, orderly laws is a contradiction. And a stipulated world with regularity and order that always helps and never hurts finite beings such as we humans are, or such as all other earthly creatures are, does not pass the test of reason. To reject or wish to flee the present world on the ground of the ambiguity of its natural laws is not only to indulge in wishful thinking. It is to indulge in irrational thinking.

I speak for myself, of course, in making these observations and do not wish to impugn or voice disrespect for anyone else's faith. I believe, however, that the reasonableness of such faith needs to be questioned and that secular criticism of this kind of thinking is justified. But not all forms of religious faith deplore or hold out the desperate hope of escape from the ambiguities of nature in the manner I am describing in this section. It is a mistake, therefore, to assume that this response is necessarily characteristic of religion as such. Religion is not synonymous with irrationality.

Nonhuman Animate Nature

It would seem to be true that plants do not have a nervous system sufficiently like that of sentient animals to consciously fear for the preservation of their lives, even though they are subject to many kinds of predation. But plants and plant species certainly do have ways of protecting themselves and one another against threats to their lives and wellbeing, and they are always in need of doing so. German forester Peter Wohlleben traces out in careful and charming detail ways in which trees protect themselves from harm as well as communicate with and give aid to one another (2017: passim). The more complex and highly developed sentient animals live lives of continual alertness to possible predators and other dangers, the greater the need to protect themselves accordingly. They are also capable of experiencing in varying degrees the suffering and loss that can result from predations against them and their kind.

Moreover, all life forms are subject to the possibility of deteriorating habitats and of endangerments and deprivations of various kinds affecting themselves and the ecosystems on which they rely. It is inevitable that they be so, in view of the fact that they must not only prey on other forms of life in order to survive but are themselves in constant danger of being preyed upon. And as Darwin points out in the passage quoted at the opening of this chapter from his groundbreaking book *The Origin of Species*, all forms of life are subject to potentially hazardous conditions of weather, drought, flooding, depletion of food and water, destructions of key parts of their habitats, and other factors of nature that threaten their lives and the lives of their progeny from season to season. Even whole species whose intricate bodily systems have evolved over vast stretches of time are in constant danger of destruction in such a world. Millions of such species that existed in the past exist no more, and millions are in grave danger of extinction today.

Nonhuman animate nature's wonders, beauties, and provocative mysteries can seem to be eclipsed by its massive tragic sufferings, sorrows, and losses. The tiny bird quivers with death pangs in the talons of the hawk, and the shiny fish wiggles helplessly in the beak of the heron. The swift gazelle is separated from its herd—felled, ripped apart, and eaten by hungry leopards or lions. And the magnificent white rhinoceros is threatened with imminent extinction in our time. A mule deer dies in the snowy winter for want of sufficient forage to keep it and its fellow deer alive until the greening of spring. Nonhuman animate nature is riddled with blood and gore, ripped and ravaged flesh, plaintive writhings in the throes of death, frantic pangs of hunger and thirst, and threats and uncertainties from all sides.

Far from being a place only of placid beauty, rest, and security, nonhuman animate nature gives evidence of also being an arena of anxious wariness, desperate struggle, unavoidable pain, and irretrievable loss. How can we cherish, revere, honor, or even come calmly to terms with a nature of ceaseless conflicts, haunting dangers, and imminent predations such as this? Is it not weighted down by dreadful ambiguities of fright, suffering, and death? Is it not "groaning in travail" for its redemption—for a future time, achingly longed for, when "the wolf shall dwell with the lamb, and the leopard shall lie down with the kid" in everlasting comfort and concord (Romans 8:23; Isaiah 11:6)?

This vision of a future peaceable kingdom of nature on earth, rid at last of such ambiguity—or at least of a heavenly realm where all ambiguity has been forever expunged—is brought into dominant focus by some religious people and religious traditions. But the vision is not a necessary feature of all religions or of all kinds of religious faith. It does not count as a credible basis for distinguishing everything sacred from all that is secular.

The question we need to ask ourselves at this point is this one: Is there a conceivable way of imagining nature rid of such ambiguity? What would nature look like when freed of predation, to say nothing of being freed of any sort of threat or uncertainty? If no predatory creatures existed, what sorts of life form would be left in nature, if any? What would they eat? How would they have evolved when there are no struggles for existence or need for finding, fashioning, or protecting particular adaptive niches in ecological systems? What would the food chain be like that channels the energy of the sun through all life forms? If all of the carnivores and omnivores ceased to exist, what would nature be converted into with absence of the present widespread diversity of flesh-eating beings? Would more be lost than gained, so far as the magnificence of nature in the present is concerned? How could we be sure that it would not?

Would even human omnivores exist, or would all humans be vegans or vegetarians by their nature? Even then, they would routinely have to destroy other life forms in order to live. What about plants and trees? Would they no longer compete with one another for sunshine, sustenance, and living space? Would no insects bore into them for food or feed on their saps and leaves? And how would insects themselves survive without needing to feast on living plants or on one another? Furthermore, would there be no such things as storms, floods, fires, earthquakes, droughts, landslides, and the like to threaten earth's living creatures?

Is it conceivable that the earth could be so rigid, unchanging, and stable, so devoid of unexpected calamities, as this scenario would require? Is it really conceivable that life as we know it could flourish on such an earth? Even more fundamentally, could biological evolution still occur and give rise to a multiplicity of diverse creatures in the absence of the continuous struggle for survival that Darwin's great work examines and describes? And if there were no such thing as death for any of earth's creatures, would the carrying capacity of our planet not long ago have been overrun, as Darwin argues?

The scenario of an entirely peaceable plant and animal world is so radically different from the nonhuman animate nature that we know as to stretch even the most elastic imaginations beyond comprehension or belief. Trying to conceive of a heavenly world to come that is devoid of all such ambiguities places similar stress on our powers of imagination. And a heavenly domain consisting only of resurrected human beings and no other kinds of earth's present life pales in comparison with the nature we experience here on earth. It would be like a cheap embroidery consisting of only one sort of thread and bereft of all but one pale color, lacking the panoplied splendor of the multiple, endlessly fascinating, radically interdependent life forms—many of them still awaiting our discovery—that we tend to take for granted here on earth. We should be careful of what we pray for and aspire toward. We could lose much more in this way than what we stand to gain. Some, but not all, religious outlooks admittedly—and I think regrettably—lack this kind of circumspection.

The Human Side of Nature

The human side of nature has been fraught with wars, pogroms, genocides, injustices, cruelties, oppressions, enslavements, murders, robberies, lies, extortions, and other human evils inflicted on humans by humans throughout human history. And we are now living in what many thinkers refer to as the Anthropocene Age, or the time in which the human species has become able to exert a dominant, all-pervading, and often oppressive influence on the earth's ecosystems and environments. This dominance has been produced by, among other things, the massive growth of the human population in recent years, with its increasing encroachments on other living beings and their habitats, and by the burgeoning developments and earth-wide utilizations of technology stemming from the Industrial Revolution. The result has been largely human caused global climate change; widespread endangerments of earth's nonhuman species; rampant ocean acidification and warming; disastrous atmospheric, riverine, and land pollution; and the like.

The evils of inhumane treatment or careless neglect by humans on one another are complemented, therefore, by the evils humans are inflicting, consciously or unconsciously, on the geological earth and its countless nonhuman forms of life. This earth is rife with moral ambiguities—human and nonhuman alike—and, in the judgment of considerable numbers of religious people, is hardly fit for human habitation. Such people, often abetted by selective aspects or interpretations of their religious scriptures and traditions, despair of life on earth and yearn for an entirely different habitation or at least a radically different earth where humans do no harm to one another or to their dwelling place but exist in unambiguous peace, painlessness, justice, and joy with one another and with all of earth's creatures. Secular critics of religion are right to regard some religions in this way, but not all religions or types of religious faith fit into this pattern.

The idea of a form of existence safeguarded against any possibility of human evils inflicted on one another, on nonhuman creatures, or on the surrounding environments of humans and nonhumans alike, is both inconceivable and undesirable. It is inconceivable because it overlooks the dynamic character of the universe, of the history of the earth, and of its finite creatures, human and nonhuman, alike. Where there are no conflicts of goods, there can be no diversities of goods. Where there is no threatening finitude, there can be no finite creatures. Where there are no natural laws that can sometimes hurt as well as harm, or help some at the expense of others, there can be no orderly mode of existence. But most fundamentally, where there is no possibility of human-inflicted evil, there can be no possibility of genuine human freedom.

And where humans are stripped of their freedom, there can be no such thing as human challenge, opportunity, or responsibility. Humans would become machines rather than persons—hardly a desirable state to be aspired toward. This would also be a kind of existence that is no longer recognizably human. Any conceivable set of natural laws must be capable of helping as well as hurting in particular circumstances, as I have shown. And genuine human freedom must always be capable of doing evil as well as good. It is certainly desirable to maximize good human choices and their influences and effects on other humans and the earthly community as a whole, and to minimize as far as possible the evil choices of human beings and the consequences of these choices. But so long as there is genuine freedom, there will remain not only the possibility but also the high probability of evil human choices and actions.

The absence of such freedom would be the absence of humanity as we know it and experience it every day. I maintain that the good of human freedom and the genuine personhood it makes possible far outweigh any conceivable avoidance of evil that its absence might seem to promise. It is the good of human freedom, moreover, that gives assurance of the formidable power to reform and mitigate—although not to forever eliminate—the admittedly dire and rampant consequences of human freedom's past and present misuses. Escape from the ambiguities and evils of finite human freedom would be nothing less than escape from humanity itself. One can be fervently religious and heartily endorse this conclusion in the name of religion. One does not have to be a secularist or to take an adamantly anti-religious stand in doing so.

Religious Affirmation of Nature

I am urging in this book recognition of the fact that not all religions insist on such features as anticipation of a timeless personal afterlife; proclamation of absolutely certain religious truths; possession of truths that stand in necessary sharp contrast with the findings of the natural and social sciences rather than existing in harmony with them when religion, on the one hand, and the methods and theories of the particular sciences, on the other, are properly understood; or revulsion toward and rejection of the ambiguities of nature in the hope of some kind of final rescue from these ambiguities in another spiritual world or in radical reconstruction of the world in which we humans presently live. Since none of these views is essential to religion, religion should not be identified with any one of them or with all of them taken together. Consequently, it would be a mistake to identify secularism simply with rejection of these views, as if they were essential to what it means to be religious or to exhibit profound religious faith.

In this section, I shall discuss examples of religious outlooks where the ambiguities of nature are welcomed and cherished rather than deplored and rejected. The first example is Daoism, the second is pantheism, and the third is religious naturalism. These outlooks are naturalistic rather than supernaturalistic; none of them believes in or gives central place to the personal God familiar to proponents of traditional Western theism; none of them lays claim to literalistically or absolutely true divine revelations; none of them denies the positive importance and value of any of the particular sciences; and none of them bemoans or aches for escape from the ambiguities of nature into some kind of immortal, painless, unthreatening existence. Yet, none of these three outlooks can rightly be regarded as implicitly nonreligious or purely *secular* responses to the world or to the lives of humans in the world.

The *Daode jing* and the *Zhuangzi* are the two major and most familiar *Daoist* texts. Here is how the former speaks of nature, under the rubric of "the ten thousand things" of the natural world:

> Tao [Dao] gave them birth;
> The "power" of Tao reared them,
> Shaped them according to their kinds,
> Perfected them, giving to each its strength,
> Therefore of the ten thousand things there is not one that
> does not worship Tao and do homage to its "power." No
> mandate ever went forth that accorded to Tao the right to
> be worshipped, nor to its "power" the right to receive homage.
> It was always and of itself so. (Waley 1958: 205)

This Dao is the "Way" of nature in all of its aspects, so it is nature that is worthy of profound religious reverence and homage, not something different from nature or more ultimate than nature. Daoism does not have a personal God, for example, that is on a higher level of religious importance than nature. Nature is the focus of Daoism as a type of religious faith. Nature is neither created nor destroyed, but its living creatures—including its human ones—experience continual creation and destruction. And this inherent Way of nature is acknowledged, welcomed, and reverenced. Furthermore, there is no dream of personal immortality or insistence that it is needed to compensate for agonies and deprivations of the ongoing world. In his introduction to the *Daode jing* (which he transliterates as *Tao Tê Ching*), British scholar Arthur Waley has this to say about the Daoist attitude toward nature:

> That we should question nature's right to make and unmake, that we should hanker after some role that nature did not intend us to play is not merely futile, not merely damaging to that tranquility of the "spirit" which is the essence of Taoism, but involves, in view of our utter helplessness, a sort of fatuity at once comic and disgraceful. . . . To be in harmony with, not in rebellion against the fundamental laws of the universe is the first step, then, on the way to Tao. (1958: 54–55)

Implicit in this outlook on nature and the place of human beings in nature is, Waley observes, an attitude toward the impending deaths of human beings that "is one not merely of resignation nor even of acquiescence, but a lyrical, almost ecstatic acceptance which has inspired some of the most moving passages in Taoist literature" (55).

There is no wistful pining here, therefore, for an afterlife of timeless or everlasting bliss as a central preoccupation of religious faith. The ambiguities of nature, which incorporate creation and destruction, accident and suffering, predation and sustenance, as well as the inescapable finality of human death, are readily welcomed and affirmed by Daoism's religious outlook on the world.

Moreover, Daoism's sacred texts lay no claim to incontestable divine revelation or absolute certainty. They are acknowledged as *human* productions, and their language—far from being abstract, doctrinal, or literal—is pervasively poetic, metaphorical, suggestive, evocative, and even playful. It firmly resists being distilled into any kind of exact, univocal statement. The purpose of this language throughout, as Daoist scholar Kuang-ming Wu notes of the other main Daoist text the *Zhuangzi*, is not abstract statements, descriptions, or prescriptions but poetic invitations to each reader or hearer to explore the meanings and applications of its suggestive, provocative, and often initially perplexing language for the reader's own life. The emphasis of this exploratory language, therefore, is on each person's self-discovery, not on putative truths handed down from supposed external authorities (1990: 367–69). The "blurred ambivalence" of the *Zhuangzi*, as well as of the *Daode jing*, says Wu, "corresponds to a real ambivalence in the nature of things whose meanings are yet to be brought forth by and in the observer. Their precise expression is produced by a poetically controlled ambivalence which responds to the concrete vagueness" of the world (369). Evocative ambiguity is thus no scandal for Daoism, either in its sacred texts, in human lives, or in nature. It is the path or Way to saving truth.

Pantheism is another religious outlook on the world in which there is no personal God, no personal immortality, and no claim to the objective, literal truth of religious texts. Instead, fervent religious fealty is given to the natural world with all of its ambiguities. This world is seen as the origin, sustainer, field of operation, and final destiny of each human life. We humans come from nature, live for a time as creatures of nature, and return to nature in our deaths. Nature is self-sustaining rather than being dependent on some principle, power, or deity outside itself. Life in nature is admittedly precarious and fraught with ambiguity, but nature is our creaturely home and the rightful focus of religious faith.

The great German Protestant theologian of the nineteenth century, Friedrich Daniel Ernst Schleiermacher, takes careful note of the religious significance of pantheism in his book entitled (in English translation) *On Religion: Speeches to Its Cultured Despisers*. He does not explicitly endorse either traditional monotheism or pantheism in this book, but he shows in illuminating detail how pantheism—and not just monotheism—can be an assuring, demanding, and empowering type of religious faith. The despisers' rejection of such things as belief in a personal God and the hope of escape from the ambiguities of nature into an allegedly perfect, entirely safe afterlife should not be viewed, therefore, as the rejection of religious faith altogether. Pantheism is an alternative kind of religion whose merits should be carefully considered by the cultured despisers of traditional, doctrinal Christian monotheism. For Schleiermacher it is a viable and important religious option, a naturalistic, this-worldly view he examines and shows the viability of throughout this book.

How does Schleiermacher conceive of pantheism and of its importance as a type of religious faith? I want to show how he does so by focusing on two aspects of pantheism on which he lays heavy emphasis. The first one is the religious ultimacy of nature rather than of a transcendent personal God regarded as the external creator and sustainer of nature. The second aspect is rejection of belief in the human survival of death in an allegedly perfect afterlife. Neither of these two conceptions is necessary to religious faith, according to Schleiermacher. They are *not* for him "the very poles and first articles of religion" (1958: 92). Pantheism as he conceives it rejects both of these conceptions but is nevertheless a deeply meaningful religious option. Rejection of traditional monotheism and belief in the afterlife should therefore not be seen as equivalent to a secularist dismissal of all religion. The cultured despisers need a more adequate understanding of the nature of religion in order to see why this is so.

The source of all true and meaningful religion for Schleiermacher is not texts, traditions, or doctrines. It is an appropriate kind of *feeling*. It is vivid awareness in the depths of one's being of the presence of the sacred or divine in the whole of nature. It is acknowledgment of the ambiguities and often seemingly chaotic disunities and disruptions of nature, but with profound feeling for the interdependency, integration, and wholeness that lie beneath and beyond them. Schleiermacher notes the unity within plurality, and the suffusive order within diverse, apparently separate and disorganized aspects of nature, in the following way:

> You see that the irregularity of the world, so often employed against religion, has really a greater value for religion than the order which is first presented to us in our study of the world and which is visible in a smaller part. The perturbations in the course of the stars point to a higher unity and a bolder combination than those we have already discovered in the regularity of their orbits. The anomalies, the idle sports of plastic Nature, compel us to see that she handles her most definite forms with free, nay capricious arbitrariness, with a phantasy the laws of which only a higher standpoint can show. (1958: 68)

A bit further on, Schleiermacher remarks that in the whole of nature "nothing simple is to be found, but all is skillfully connected and interwoven" (70). A reflective sense of the whole that lies beneath all of the particularities of nature is for him a revelation—when registered in the depths of human feeling—of what he calls the Spirit of the World. Attunement to this World-Spirit in firsthand human feeling and awareness is for Schleiermacher what it means to be religious, whether that World-Spirit is thought to be a personal deity or an immanent presence and power pervading the world. The idea of a personal God is thus not essential to religion but only one way of thinking about religion.

In any event, the seat of religion is in feeling for Schleiermacher, not in particular ideas or beliefs. It is important to see, however, that by *feeling* (*Gefühl*) he does not mean mere emotion but heartfelt, firsthand recognition of deep religious truth and incorporation of this felt truth into the entirety of one's life. It is in such personal feeling and appropriation, not in external doctrines or beliefs that authentic religion resides. The feeling of reverence and love for the whole of nature that lies behind the multiplicity of its particular aspects, and of one's self as an intimate part of this whole, is of critical importance to Schleiermacher as "the germ of all the religious feelings furnished by this side of existence" (71).

Such feeling can for Schleiermacher be every bit as much the basis of pantheistic faith as it is of monotheistic faith. By it, the existence of God is disclosed, whether God be conceived in theistic or pantheistic terms. "Is it not God alone before whom and in whom all particular things disappear? And if you see the world as a Whole, a Universe, can you do it otherwise than in God?" he asks rhetorically (94). He then goes on to note the perennial resistance, even in theistic religion, to conceiving of God anthropomorphically, that is, as a particular "thinking and willing Person," and how a more adequate conception of "the Highest Being" is of that Being as "exalted above all personality as the universal, productive, connecting necessity of all thought and existence" (95). Viewed in this way, the distinction between theism and pantheism is greatly attenuated, at least for Schleiermacher.

If we turn from Schleiermacher's conception of God in *On Religion* to his view of immortality, we find that it is not the hope of personal immortality or continuing life beyond death that he emphasizes but the immortality we can have in our present temporal life. He scorns the idea of a personal immortal afterlife as an impious, irreligious focus on oneself instead of on "God wherein all that is individual and fleeting disappears" (100). The kind of immortality of which he strongly approves, he characterizes in this way: "It is the immortality which we can now have in this temporal life; it is the problem in the solution of which we are forever to be engaged. In the midst of finitude to be one with the Infinite and in every moment to be eternal is the immortality of religion" (101). This conception of immortality is consistent with a piety toward the whole of nature, a whole of which we individual humans are only a small part. Schleiermacher's conceptions of nature as a whole, of God, and of authentic religious feeling show them to be consistent with either a pantheistic or a sufficiently modified theistic outlook on the world. Our concern here has been his elucidation of the nature of pantheism as a genuinely religious perspective and thus as a perspective that has to be included in any adequate contrast between religion and secularity.

The third religious outlook I want to draw into this discussion is religious naturalism. The seventeenth-century philosopher Baruch (or Benedict de) Spinoza is probably the best-known exponent of a type of this view. In his *Ethics* he famously identifies nature with God, speaking of "the eternal and infinite Being, which we call God or Nature" (1955: pt. 4, p. 188). But the view is also represented in the various kinds of religious naturalism that have come to be increasingly developed and presented in more recent years. I will discuss here some main themes of religious naturalism. Daoism and pantheism can be viewed as versions of religious naturalism in that both conceive of nature as religiously ultimate in the sense of manifesting or containing the Way or God as their fundamental religious focus and principle. The version of religious naturalism that I shall now briefly describe, however, focuses simply on nature in all of its aspects as the object of religious reverence and sustaining faith. Nature as a whole is not said to be identical with God or to have God or some sort of divine beings as its central religious aspects. My intent here as elsewhere in this book is to stress the wide range of available religious outlooks and to warn against too narrow assumptions about the nature of religion in exploring the differences between religion and secularity.

For religious naturalism, every mode of existence is natural. Nature is all there is. There are no supernatural beings, realms, principles, or powers. There is no ground of nature that enables it to be what it is. Nature is its own ground, and the ground of all existence, past, present, and future. Humans are biological organisms. They have no immaterial souls, and they are born and fated to die just like all other biological organisms. Hence, there is no such thing as personal immortality. Humans are integral parts of nature and have both the privilege and the responsibility of being good citizens of the community comprised of all other natural beings, together with their earthly habitats and ecological interdependencies. The religious meaning of humans' lives and their individual and collective salvation consist in the sense of their being at home in nature, attuned to the rhythms, wonders, and mysteries of nature, living lives of reverence and responsibility toward nature, and experiencing the inspirations and empowerments of nature in every aspect of their lives. Religious naturalism welcomes the findings of the natural and social sciences as contributing in crucial ways to this religious sensibility. And it accepts the partiality and probabilistic character of all claims to truth, including its own religious claims. It does not lay claim to any absolute certainties.

The ambiguities of nature are accepted and affirmed by religious naturalism as the necessary accompaniments of nature's dynamic processes, its ongoing creations and destructions whereby older things pass out of being as new things come into being. The ambiguities also result from the radical interdependencies of its creatures as they interact with one another in order to make common use of the energy of the sun and in this way to maintain their respective forms of life on earth. This interaction is recognized to be as crucial for humans as it is for other earthly species. Humans are not viewed in religious naturalism as the apex of nature here on earth, much less in the universe as a whole, but only as one of earth's millions of evolved species.

Humans do have the gift, however, of a level of conscious awareness of nature and of their place on earth—as well as an ability to develop and articulate this conscious awareness linguistically—that is unique to their species. This ability, along with their capacity of genuine freedom—lies behind their remarkable technical prowess. It gives them the ambiguous power to do much good on earth, but also to do great harm to every aspect of the earth and its other creatures. A keen sense of ecological awareness and responsibility is thus a central part of the felt responsibility and demand of religious naturalism. Humans also have the power to exercise their freedom in their interactions with one another, and the two-edged character of the sword of this freedom accounts for both the blessings and harms they are capable of bringing to or inflicting on members of their own species.

Human institutions and culturally instilled patterns of life can aid or help in this regard, and religious naturalism is deeply concerned with the importance of working to ensure that they support justice and peace instead of contributing to needless conflicts and harms among humans and among all of earth's creatures. The assurance of being at home here on the material earth and not belonging to some other purely spiritual realm, the demand of being a responsible citizen of the community of all of the earth's creatures, the urgent need to use the gifts of consciousness and freedom in ways to enhance instead of detracting from the natural health and beauty of the earth, the continuing, ever-developing reverence for the sacredness of the earth and of the whole vast universe—all of these are matters of professed and profound religious significance for religious naturalism. Nature is all there is, but it is more than enough to be the amply assuring, demanding, and empowering focus of authentic religious faith. This is the creed of religious naturalism. It is a creed that thankfully accepts and affirms the ambiguities of nature as necessary to nature's religious majesty and ultimacy.

Conclusion

In this chapter I discussed the ambiguities of inanimate nature, animate, nonhuman nature, and the human side of nature. I showed why these ambiguities are inevitable because of the essential role of natural laws in nature; because of the struggles of organisms to adapt to and maintain their places in the food chains and other aspects of the intricate ecological systems of earth; and because of the ability of humans to do either good or evil in the world with their remarkable gift of freedom. I argued that secular thinkers are right in their criticisms of religious thinkers who deplore these ambiguities, but that they are wrong in assuming that *all* religious people despair of these necessary ambiguities and anxiously yearn for release from them by transformation into some other realm or state of being.

In support of the latter thesis, I showed how the religious outlooks of Daoism, pantheism, and religious naturalism, for example, willingly accept and affirm the ambiguities of nature and enjoin a grateful reverence toward all of nature and for the place of humans in nature. They do so by acknowledging that humans are at home in nature and are integral parts of the community of other creatures of nature, instead of seeing humans as destined for a home beyond nature in some kind of immortal afterlife.

Not all kinds of religion, then, can be distinguished from all kinds of secularism on the ground that the former necessarily deplore the ambiguities of nature, see humans as spiritual beings separate in their true character from material nature, and regard them as having their true home in a state or realm beyond or other than the natural one. Gladly *recognizing* and taking *responsibility* for the role of humans in nature rather than seeking desperately for escape from nature are therefore the bywords for these three examples of religious responses to the ambiguities of nature. Secular affirmations of nature can thus be accompanied by religious ones, meaning that the distinction between the two cannot convincingly be based on their respective responses to these ambiguities.

After all, the ambiguities point in two directions, not just one. They are not just inevitable; they are in countless ways welcome and desirable. In fact, it is difficult if not impossible to conceive of a world devoid of them or to imagine that such a world would be more desirable than the natural world in which we humans are privileged currently to live. Our focus should be on assuming responsible roles as citizens of this earth and members of the community of all of the earth's creatures. In emphasizing this idea, I anticipate the focus of the next chapter.

Chapter Five

An Urgent Common Cause

> As we wait for NASA's Insight Mission to sift through Martian sands, drilling under the red planet's terrain for life, there is a certain irony that life on our own planet is increasingly vulnerable to anthropogenic changes. No matter how advanced our technical capacities for space travel, our first call to action must be to preserve Earth.
>
> —Priyamvada Natarajan (2019: 41).

In our attempts to understand the differences between the sacred and the secular, or between religion and secularity, we should not lose sight of the critical importance of recognizing and acting on issues for which these two outlooks have, or by all indications should have, a common urgent concern and responsibility. Chief among these issues, in my view, is the fact of widespread, increasingly devastating global climate change and habitat destruction, and their multiple threats to most if not all current species of life on earth, including our own human civilization and human species. As exciting and impressive for its imagined long-range consequences as space travel is today, its prospect pales in immediate importance when compared with the urgency of our addressing in as many relevant ways possible the largely human-caused or anthropogenic catastrophe that threatens our planet earth in the current century.

This point is made with striking succinctness and force in the epigraph to this chapter quoted from of an article on the twentieth-century discovery of what scientists now regard as the dwarf planet Pluto, that refers to the amazing twentieth-first-century photographs of Pluto taken by the New Horizons spacecraft, and that raises the question of whether and to what extent we should devote our planning and energies toward the colonization of other parts of our solar system. The article is by Priyamvada Natarajan, a professor in the Departments of Astronomy and Physics at Yale University, where she also directs the Franke Program in Science and the Humanities. She wisely warns us to keep our priorities straight, a message that needs to be heard by secular and religious people alike.

In the previous chapter, I discussed three religious outlooks that give their principal attention to nature and the immanent sacredness of nature rather than to some transcendent domain or destination believed to exist outside of or beyond nature. The three religious outlooks discussed there are pantheism, Daoism, and religious naturalism, and their main preoccupation is with what we today speak of as the geological features, nonhuman life forms and ecosystems, and ecologically dependent human communities of this earth. The urgent priority Natarajan insists on is already implicit in these three religious outlooks. In view of their central preoccupation with nature, Natarajan's priority comes "naturally" to each of them. For them, heartfelt reverence for nature and strong sense of responsibility for the continuing well-being of nature are tightly conjoined.

I want in this chapter to make reference to some examples of other ways to respond positively and effectively to the ecological crisis of our time. The first is the more traditional Western, monotheistic response of Christian spokesman Jim Antal. The second is the response of the Buddhist Eco-Dharma Centre in Spain. The third is the scientific responses of biologists Stuart A. Kauffman and E. O. Wilson. The fourth, fifth, and sixth responses are prudential, moral, and aesthetic.

A Monotheistic Response

Religious responses to global climate change, habitat devastation, endangered species, and the like on the part of more traditional religious outlooks and communities are beginning to find powerful expression in our time. The Reverend Jim Antal is a denominational leader of the United Church of Christ who serves as a spokesman for climate change on behalf of the denomination. His 2018 book *Climate Church, Climate World: How People of Faith Must Work for Change* is a clarion call for urgent, far-reaching attention by Christians, other religious groups, and humanity as a whole to the onrushing ecological crisis of our century.

"No longer is it morally adequate," Antal writes, "to expand our understanding of justice to include in the circle of neighborly treatment more distant neighbors. We must recognize that all people, indeed all creatures alive and those yet to be born, are our neighbors." He continues in this spirit, saying,

> God is calling us to reorient our hearts, our lives, and our laws so that we honor and respect the interdependence of all of creation. We are called to confess the harm our generation has done to the Earth and to future generations. Such honesty and repentance can set us free to take action that will help future generations to survive, perhaps even to thrive. (59)

Antal stresses the urgency of prompt and effective attention to the ecological crisis by Christians and others when he observes that "climate disruption is amplifying all the other injustices. Our efforts to advance God's mission and to build a just world at peace are undermined by the fact that Earth's life systems are no longer stable" (57).

His attitude as a Christian stands in stark contrast to the attitude of Senator James Inhofe of Oklahoma, who was quoted in a March 9, 2012, interview with Brad Johnson as saying, "As long as the Earth remains, there will be seedtime and harvest, cold and heat, winter and summer, day and night." He then went on to assert, "My point is, God is still up there. The arrogance of people to think that we, human beings, would be able to change what He (God) is doing is to me outrageous." Inhofe is convinced, in other words, that global warming is not an imminent threat but a ridiculous hoax (Johnson 2012; also quoted in Antal 2018: 18–19).

It is important for us to recognize that it is not just those with the religious outlooks of Daoism, pantheism, and religious naturalism that revere nature and are concerned with the ecological crisis. *Monotheists* like Antal are also deeply worried about this crisis and anxious to find effective ways of responding to it. Many of them may also believe, as he does, that there is a heavenly afterlife that awaits faithful Christians,[1] but such ecologically minded theists do not emphasize this belief at the expense of our responsibility to care for our natural home here and now. Ecological justice for all of nature's creatures and not just a justice focused only on humans—even though humans are profoundly involved in it—is their strong concern. Antal's book is a passionate defense of this thesis. He draws fully on the resources of the Christian tradition in developing his defense. His book is being recognized, read, and taken to heart by many of today's thoughtful Christians.

A Buddhist Response

The Buddhist Eco-Dharma Center, located high in the Catalan Pyrenees Mountains,[2] exemplifies a growing sense of ecological responsibility and action among engaged Buddhists. The center's programs are devoted to developing an ecological consciousness rooted in the traditional Buddhist stress on the interconnectedness of all things, a stress captured in the central doctrine of *Śūnyatā pratityasamutpāda*. This doctrine takes issue with the notion of independent, substantial existence, including the supposed existence of a substantial human self: hence, the Buddhist doctrine of *Śūnyatā* or "emptiness." It emphasizes instead the codependent arising and ceasing of all things (*pratityasamutpāda*)—a conception suggestive of the interdependent ecological web of birth, life, and death characterizing all creatures in nature.

This interconnectedness is represented, among other ways, in the Hua-Yen, Mahayana Buddhist use of the symbol of Indra's Net—a symbol of central importance to the Eco-Dharma Centre. Indra's Net is a web-like fabric that encompasses the whole universe and incorporates a precious jewel at each of its innumerable points of connection. Each jewel is a unique perspective on all of the other perspectives that are included in the net. The net can symbolize the interwoven interdependencies of all ecological niches and of all the particular creatures making their livings in these niches. Each creature has a responsible, compassionate, unselfcentered (*Śūnyatā*) relation to other creatures in the earth-wide ecological web, and this idea can be interpreted to include all the human creatures in nature. The Jeweled Net of Indra is an evocative symbol of ecological interdependencies that are remarkably resilient but not immune to endangerment and destruction. The Eco-Dharma Centre is wise to make use of this symbol as a way of calling attention to our pressing need for ecological awareness and responsibility.

Scientific Responses

Reverence for the sacredness of nature is also the fundamental motif of the 2008 book by biologist Stuart A. Kauffman entitled *Reinventing the Sacred: A New View of Science, Reason, and Religion*. Kauffman proposes that we "reinvent" the concept of the sacred, as well as the traditional Western conception of God, and that we do so along the lines of emergentist science. We can do so, he insists, by identifying God, not with a transcendent creator of nature, but with the immanent creativity of nature itself, as reflected in the inherent dynamisms of the abiotic universe, the biosphere, and humanity. For Kauffman, the universe is only partially a universe of rigorous natural laws—a view of it expressed in the causally deterministic physics of Galileo and Newton, and axiomatized in the philosophy of Spinoza. The natural laws of the universe have enabled but not determined nature's novel creations over billions of years—creative upsurgings of many different kinds that are especially evident in earth's history of biological evolution.

This natural creativity is also apparent in the history of human beings and their cultural achievements. Kauffman boldly suggests that religion is part of these emergent human cultural achievements. All of religion without exception gives evidence of *human* creativity for him, not of the creations of a transcendent divine being, of any sort of wisdom and truth handed down by such a being, or of any other transcendent, nonnatural source. The focus of the concept of the sacred, therefore, should be on nature itself—as well as on human beings and their cultural histories and traditions as integral manifestations of nature's immanent creativity.

Seen in this way, Kauffman proposes that we call this natural creativity, the profuse evolutionary emergentism witnessed throughout nature, *God*. He proposes this term to designate the sacredness of nature in all of its aspects of natural laws, an evolving cosmos, our solar system, earth, life forms on earth, and the evolution of human beings and their cultural creations. He defends this proposal in the following way:

> Do we use the word *God* meaning that God is the natural creativity of the universe? We are not forced to do so. It may not be wise. This use of the word *God* is open to angry misinterpretation, for we have reserved this word in the Abrahamic tradition to refer to the Creator God. How dare we use the word *God* to stand for the natural creativity in the universe? Yet I say yes, we can and should choose to do so, knowing full well that we make this choice. No other human symbol carries millennia of awe and reverence. (2008: 284)

I think that Kauffman is mistaken in claiming that no other symbol carries as much awe and reverence as the God symbol, because it does not do justice to the powerful symbolisms of nontheistic religious traditions such as Daoism, Theravada Buddhism, and Advaita Vedanta Hinduism. Nevertheless, his call for recognizing the sacredness of nature in all of its aspects is entirely appropriate and even necessary for us in our time of ecological crisis.

With such a reinvention of the sacred, Kauffman contends, we will be able to find common ground "across our diverse traditions, religious and cultural" and to work to produce a "shared sacred and make it a safe space for all of us." He sees this process as providing the hope of healing "the split between reason and faith." What he discusses in his book, he asserts, "is a science, a world view, and a God with which we can live our lives forward forever into mystery" (286, 288). Thus what he envisions is a breaking down of the distinction between religion and secularity with a deeply inspiring, widely shared, powerfully motivating sense of the sacred that can cut across this distinction.

With its focus on the whole of nature, the worldview he proposes has obvious critical bearing on our present ecological crisis. For far too long, we humans have tended to see nature as subservient to us rather than seeing ourselves as being responsible to the nature from which we have emerged as biological organisms and on which we crucially depend. Kauffman's vision of the sacrality of nature's creativity is a welcome counterforce to this calamitous tendency. Religious and nonreligious people can lay claim to the sacredness of nature as a conviction that brings them together rather than dividing them. This sacredness can be articulated and developed in a wide variety of both religious and secular ways, showing that the two approaches are not necessarily as separate or distinct as we tend commonly to assume. Religion does, however accord an explicit ontological status and importance to the sacred that secular perspectives as such do not. I shall explain and defend this difference between the two outlooks in the next chapter.

I want now, however, to venture three caveats to Kauffman's thesis. One relates to his conception of faith. The second relates to the diversity of both religious and secular outlooks on the world. The third relates to his use of the term *God* to designate the creativity of nature. First, Kauffman assumes without argument, as shown by the quotation in the previous paragraph, that the term *faith* means something distinct from reason, opposed to reason, or split off from reason. He does not recognize that there is such a thing as faithful reason or that reason is undergirded by stances of faith. But I believe that deep-lying postures of faith *underlie all reason* and therefore that we should not distinguish between religion and secularity by arguing that faith belongs solely to religion and not to secular outlooks as well. What Kauffman is proposing, in my view then, is *a new kind of faith* that can possibly be seen as a driving force of both religion and secularity, namely, a faith in the sacredness of nature.[3]

This faith does not require abandoning all traditional theistic conceptions of God, because a profound reverence for nature as God's creation is also present, more often than not, in these conceptions. Viewing the earth as the creation of God can enhance its sacrality and need not detract from it. "The earth is the Lord's, and the fullness thereof; / The world and they that dwell therein," sings the psalmist in the Jewish and Christian scriptures (Psalm 24:1; *Holy Scriptures* 1952 [Jewish Publication Society translation]). And the Qur'an declares, "The seven heavens and the earth and everyone in them glorify Him [Allah]. There is not a single thing that does not celebrate His praise . . ." (17:44; *Qur'an* 2015 [Haleem translation]).

In the *second* place, therefore, the commonality of recognizing the sacredness of nature that Kauffman dreams of need not be monolithic or purely scientific. It can be pluralistic and diverse, taking into account many different religious and secular outlooks. Kauffman does not seem to me to take sufficient account of this idea in his plea for widespread acknowledgment of and commitment to the sacredness of nature. His perspective should not be seen as a wholesale "either-or," but as a "both-and" position. It can allow for and incorporate many different interpretations and approaches to the sacredness of nature, both religious and secular.

Despite these two reservations, Kauffman's emphasis on the sacredness, mystery, and wonder of nature's creativity is welcome and appropriate when considered as implying an urgent call to ecological awareness and responsibility. I remember some years ago—in a time when philosophical nihilism was in the air as the result of the ravages of two world wars, the horrors of the Holocaust, the development and recent use of nuclear weapons in the bombing of Japan, the rise of French existentialism, and other factors—seeing a cartoon with someone holding up a sign inscribed with the question "Is Nothing Sacred?" Whether or not nothingness is sacred to nihilists, I submit, along with Kauffman, that if the earth is not sacred for us humans, then nothing is, because all that we hold dear is dependent on the health and flourishing of our planetary home.

The earth is surely sacred in this way, at least in the sense of the term *sacred* that Kauffman describes as deserving "an immense respect and reverence" (286). But such respect for and conviction of deep responsibility toward nature are not confined to religious views of the world, although they are frequently associated with them. They can also be part of a secular view of the world that need not incorporate the term *God*, whether conceived as personal or impersonal, into their purview. Moreover, not all religious perspectives on the world involve the idea of God as the central focus of their forms of faith. This, then, is my *third* critical response to Kauffman's otherwise excellent book.

The mystery, wonder, and immense value of the natural world can be celebrated by religious and secular, theistic and nontheistic people alike, and it must be celebrated in thought, feeling, and action if we are to avert imminent environmental calamity and chaos. For example, the eminent biologist E. O. Wilson is profoundly disturbed by the rate of endangerments and extinctions of biological organisms in our time. He has devoted his life primarily to the study of ants, and he notes in a March 12, 2016, *New York Times* article that he has described about 450 new species of *ant* in his own lifetime—a feat that in itself testifies to his lifelong ardent love for nature. He argues that "disappearance of natural habitat is the primary cause of biological diversity loss at every level" and that the "only way to save upward of 90 percent of the rest of life is to vastly increase the area of refuges, from their currently 15 percent of land and 3 percent of the sea to *half of the land and half of the sea*" (my italics). Wilson then proposes a way of accomplishing this arduous, extremely demanding goal and concludes, "This step toward sustained coexistence with the rest of life is partly a practical challenge and partly a moral decision. It can be done, and to great and universal benefit, if we wish it so."

There is a pervasive moral tone to Wilson's argument, but no mention of religion. However, he exhibits here and elsewhere in his life and writings what can be called a profound, loving, awesome respect for the natural world. Wilson's argument, with its emphasis on practicality and morality, anticipates the sections to follow on prudential and moral reasons for being alert to, urgently concerned with, and actively seeking effective ways to react to the rapidly growing ecological crisis of our time.

Can his scientifically informed respect be called "secular"? I think it can, and what we see when we compare and contrast the various views indicated so far in this chapter—and especially those of Kauffman and Wilson—is a mounting confluence of the sacred and the secular that leaves us still with the problem of how accurately and adequately to distinguish the distinctively religious sense of the term *sacred* from secular uses of this term, or at least from strong secular suggestions of the term's more general, colloquial meanings and applications.

We in the United States can revere as sacred our national Constitution, for example. We can revere our Founding Fathers in this way. We can revere as sacred the memory of our departed parents, siblings, teachers, colleagues, and friends. We can revere the Lincoln Memorial, the Washington Monument, the Statue of Liberty, and our national flag. We can revere those who struggled and fought to make our present liberties possible. To revere these and many other things, including the natural world, is in some real sense to hold them *sacred*. But it is not necessarily to do so in a *religious* sense of this term. Examination of the latter, and of its contrast with the *secular*, requires our further careful investigation, a task we shall continue to pursue throughout this book.

In the meantime, I want to inquire further into reasons for which we humans might be concerned with and be intent on acting in relation to the ecological crisis *apart from* religious reasons or at least *in addition to* religious reasons. This inquiry can help to sharpen our perception of the difference between a religious and a secular outlook on the world by helping us to better understand what the term *secular* can be taken to include and mean. The first positively engaged response to the looming environmental crisis we can mention is *prudential*. The second is *moral*. And the third is *aesthetic*. None of these three is necessarily connected with religion, although each of them can be and frequently is so connected. The absence of necessary connection with religion means that each of them can be regarded, when not so connected, as a secular response to the environmental crisis.

Prudential Responses

We saw that E. O. Wilson uses the terms *practical* and *moral* when noting reasons for our being deeply concerned with the ecological crisis of our day. The term *prudential* is a rough synonym for the term *practical*. We need not think in moral terms when appeal is made to prudential ones. And whether or not we introduce religious considerations into our concern for the well-being of our planet or not, such concern is still urgently called for and amply justified. It is so because our own well-being is intimately tied to the well-being of the ecological systems of earth.

Global climate change, for example, threatens dangerous sea level rise, devastating floods, storms, wildfires, desertifications, rampant human and animal migrations, food and water shortages, and the like. And these have direct consequences for our human well-being, for the maintenance of our present social institutions and ways of life, for human civilization, and perhaps even for our survival as a species. The traits of rapidly impending ecological changes cannot be ignored, no matter how much we may seek to ignore them, because they are beginning to have increasing practical effects that call at the very least for well thought-out prudential responses. These effects are ignored at our imminent human peril. They can have ominous snowball effects or produce unanticipated phase transitions that, once underway, become much more difficult, if not at some point impossible, to check.

One need not be religious, particularly moral in one's outlook on the world, or deeply attuned to the aesthetic dimensions of nature to be subjected to the effects of climate change or other unavoidable symptoms of impending ecological doom. We see these effects in the melting glaciers and icefields of our mountains and polar regions; the growing acidification and warming of our oceans; rising sea levels; the dying of coral and its attendant forms of aquatic life; the emission into the atmosphere of mounting amounts of methane and carbon dioxide from melting permafrost; the increasing intensity of hurricanes, floods, and wildfires; the depletion of arable land and potable water; the perceptible effects on plant and animal life; and the like.

Yet we continue recklessly to burn fossil fuels that add carbon to the atmosphere and reflect in that way growing levels of heat back onto the earth—the same earth on which we humans must depend in order to flourish and survive. It could not be clearer that what we humans must do, and do with urgent and utmost care, is to cease ignoring the dire warnings of ecological disaster and work together to mitigate, minimize, and prevent their effects as much as humanly possible before it is too late.

This is an eminently prudential concern. It does not have to come clothed in religious, moral, or aesthetic finery to command our urgent attention. The naked practical truth should be quite enough. And it should command the intense respect, focused awareness, and active involvement of us all. Massive, fundamental, far-reaching *structural* changes throughout the earth are required, and not just raising the consciousness of individual persons, important and essential as that also is. Resources and incentives of all types—religious, scientific, moral, aesthetic, economic, political, and prudential must be brought immediately and effectively into play. We dare not underestimate the magnitude of the task that lies before us.

Moral Responses

Prudential considerations are generally restricted to a particular person or collection of persons. "How does a course of action affect me or those near to me?" is the typical prudential question. But the scope of all of the great moral theories such as virtue theory, utilitarianism, rights theory, Kantian moral theory, the Rawlsian theory of justice, and the like, is universal—at least so far as members of the human species are concerned. According to what philosopher Kurt Baier calls "the moral point of view," individual persons or groups of persons are not morally entitled at any time or in any situation to treat themselves as the exclusive or even the principal *focus* of moral obligation, or as *exceptions* to moral obligations in some or all situations that are commonly thought to apply to others (1969: 187–213).

Ethical egoism or the sole recourse to prudential considerations assumed to apply only to one's personal prospects or well-being in particular situations, mark the antithesis of the moral point of view. In other words, the moral point of view applies to everyone, not just to me or to those close to me or familiar to me. There is no relevant moral reason to consider myself as deserving of some sort of special moral considerability or treatment that does not apply to others. The moral point of view is enshrined in the Golden Rule, whether in its positive form of doing to others as I would wish that they would do to me, or its negative form of not inflicting on others practices that I would not wish for them to inflict on me. One need not be religious, or religious in any avowed sense, to be moral. Secular people and secular communities are quite capable of being moral in Baier's sense of the term—and not just prudential or self-seeking—in their patterns of thought, conviction, and practice.

What does all of this have to do with responses to the ecological crisis? It means that immediate moral concern for the effects of this crisis must be extended to all the peoples of the earth, and not just to those of one's own community or nation. We humans must work together to ensure, as far as is humanly possible, the survival and flourishing of human beings in all parts of the world, and thus to protect them from environmental disasters that affect their food and water supplies, their homes, their arable land, their heat indexes, their overpopulations, and their general conditions of life. It is of considerable moral significance to note that the environmental crisis affects more immediately and urgently those far less responsible for producing it—at least for a time—than it does those in industrial nations most responsible for it. All of us humans are in this crisis together, and we are morally obligated to our fellow humans everywhere.

But does the universality of appropriate moral considerability and concern extend only to human beings? I think that we need seriously to expand the moral point of view to include all of the creatures of the earth and their physical environments. Their flourishing and well-being, and that of their habitats and ecosystems, should also fall within the orbit of the moral point of view. It is not only humans that are all in this together, so far as the ecological crisis is concerned. It is all of the living beings of earth, human and nonhuman alike, and their countless environmental settings. The earth is our body, as it were, and to harm or destroy any critical part of our body is ultimately to harm and destroy ourselves. Increasingly polluting the earth's atmosphere, for example, has effects analogous to polluting the human body with destructive substances. People of religious and secular persuasions need to face up to this inescapable truth and to react to the global environmental crisis with profound moral conviction and concern.

This is clearly a common moral cause for us humans and it pertains to all of the denizens of earth, all of their habitats, and all of their ecosystems. It is a morality that applies to the earth's biosphere as a whole and to all of the nonliving components and systems that make its existence possible—a point reminiscent of Schleiermacher's exposition of pantheism's reverence for the *whole of nature* as in some sense divine. Plains, mountains, atmosphere, oceans, rivers, rocks, minerals, deserts, glaciers, ice floes—all these things and more are essential parts of the earth's wholeness and must be included in the scope of our moral concern for its continuing well-being. Extending the moral point of view to include all of nature here on earth would seem to require something closely akin to Schleiermacher's all-encompassing respect and reverence. An adequate ecological ethics must be a planetary ethics. It lays heavy moral responsibility on all human persons, institutions, societies, and nations, whether these be religious or secular in their dominant character.

Aesthetic Responses

Many years ago, I stood on the tundra high in Colorado's Rocky Mountain National Park. The elevation was about 12,000 feet. The summer sun was shining brightly, and the ground was decorated with tiny alpine wildflowers of different kinds. From my place on the tundra, I was able to gaze far below me at a forest of evergreen trees that swept the valley as far as the eye could see. Peaks of mountains loomed in the distance. As I stood, resting temporally from the labor of hiking at the high altitude, I was invigorated and inspired by the natural beauty surrounding me. I was experiencing the earth aesthetically, and I felt a powerful compulsion to honor and respect it. The experience was so moving and so long lasting that I still remember it vividly after many years. It had overtones of religion and morality, but the impression it made on me at that time was primarily aesthetic.

At another time, I was traveling over a highway at an elevation of about 11,000 feet in Colorado when I witnessed the remnant of a mountain top that had been scrapped off in the process of mining the mountain for its metals. The remnant was botched with multicolored liquids left over from the mining. It was an offensive, obnoxious sight. I felt a pang of deep regret for this violation of nature's natural beauty and for the continuing pollution of ground and nearby water courses the mountain top removal had left behind. My aesthetic sensibility was violated. As result I was stirred with compassion for the earth and troubled by the careless, rampant human violations of the earth's natural splendor and integrity that this experience triggered and brought sadly to mind.

Aesthetic experience and expression involve not only exaltation and beauty but also tragedy and ugliness. Both are fundamental parts of our experience as humans. Dante Alighieri's *Divine Comedy*, for example, portrays in extended detail the joys of paradise, the sufferings of purgatory, and the agonies of hell. The history of painting encompasses both the serene beauty of John Constable's English landscapes and the writhing, wretched struggle of the survivors in Theodore Gericault's painting *The Raft of the Medusa*. Edvard Munch's desperate painting *The Scream* is a treasured work of art. William Shakespeare's superb plays include *A Midsummer Night's Dream* and *Hamlet*. Leo Tolstoy's greatest novel is entitled *War and Peace*, and it lives up to its name.

The two mountaintop experiences I have just described illustrate the fact that aesthetic experience can contain elements of the beautiful and the ugly, the sublime and the wretched. The first experience was of a resplendent nature relatively untouched and unspoiled by human beings. In it, nature's evocative wonder and beauty shone forth, and as a consequence, I was filled with elation for the privilege of happening upon and contemplating a stirring example of them. I also felt on that occasion a yearning for us humans to honor, care for, and protect as far as humanly possible the beautiful and bountiful earth that is our natural home.

The second experience was also one of aesthetic significance. The repugnance it aroused had a similar effect on my ecological consciousness. Its shock evoked a searing sense of remorse for our widespread human defilements of nature and a renewed awareness of our imperative need to find ways of practicing loving and effective care for the flourishing of nature throughout the earth. Thus not only considerations of prudence and moral duty, but also attitudes prompted by aesthetic sensibility can contribute profoundly to ecological awareness and responsibility.

One can be prudentially motivated, morally stimulated, and aesthetically moved toward an urgent sense of care for the well-being of the earth without being avowedly religious or connected with any particular religious community or tradition. And one can be profoundly religious and also prudential, moral, and aesthetic in one's responses to the ecological crisis. Secular and religious people can rightly regard this issue as a common cause. No line between the secular and the religious can be generally or convincingly drawn on this basis.

Conclusion

In this chapter I considered the claim that while some religious people tend to exhibit little concern for the integrity and well-being of the earth's geological and ecological systems in their intense preoccupation with the hope of salvation after death and unshakable confidence in divine rule and protection, secular people's acceptance of our finite existence here on earth allows and can impel them to have profound regard for the ecological crisis confronting the earth. I showed that, while this conception of religion does apply to proponents of some religious outlooks, it is far from applying to all those who espouse particular forms of religious faith. I cited an example of a Christian monotheist who is working passionately for ecological awareness and responsibility in our time of imminent ecological danger and who has written a detailed book about our present ecological crisis from the perspective of Christian faith.

I also cited the example of engaged Buddhism's Eco-Dharma Centre in Spain, with its focus on the radical interconnectedness of every aspect of earth's network of life and its environs—and on humans' duty to this ecological network as integral parts of it with distinctive powers to affect it for good or ill. And I took note of two scientists' ways of giving fervent attention to our urgent need to respect and honor the earth, and to act in such a manner as to effectively address its ecological deprivations and despoliations.

The idea that religionists and secularists can share in ecological awareness and responsibility was further reinforced in the chapter by my taking account of prudential, moral, and aesthetic ways of responding with appropriate care and concern to the crises of climate change; water, ground, and air pollution; depletion of available food and water; destruction of ecological habitats; and rampant endangerment of biological species that currently inhabit the earth, including the human species.

Like it or not, religious people and secular people alike share in the common cause of actively attending to the health and well-being of the earth and its creatures. Not only do their own flourishing and even their own possible survival depend on their joint active engagements in this cause; so does that of their fellow creatures. Humans are both crucially dependent on and inescapably responsible for the web of life here on earth, and there are multiple reasons for having an anxious and urgent concern for the continuing resilience and strength of this web in all of its aspects.

Some of these reasons are religious, and others are secular; some are prudential, and others moral. Some are aesthetic responses to the soul-stirring beauties and ominous tragedies of life on earth. To seek the good and avoid the evil for earth and its creatures in every way possible is our challenge and responsibility as human beings. This task excludes neither religionists nor secularists. We are involved in it together. Our premises may differ in particular ways, but they lead ultimately and unavoidably to this common conclusion.

Chapter Six

Characterizing Religion

> One aspect [of religion] concerns *why* a belief is held and a practice done, the functional or pragmatic aspect of religion. The other aspect concerns *what* the beliefs and practices are about, the substantive or ontological aspect of religion. If one does not insist on a pure functionalist or a pure substantive definition, then one can see that the two can overlap, in the sense that a belief or a practice or an institution can be both functionally religious (providing certain kinds of benefits) and also substantively religious (concerning certain kinds of realities).
>
> —Kevin Schilbrack (2013: 297–98)

So far in this book we have seen that a number of possible ways of distinguishing religion and secularity, or what I shall ultimately term the *sacred* and the *secular*, do not work, largely because the assumed nature of religion that is operative in these distinctions is too narrow.

Not all religions or forms of religious faith uphold belief in a timeless or everlasting afterlife as the central focus and aim of their systems of thought, for example. Not all religions focus on some kind of personal deity or deities. Not all insist on the absolute, exclusive, infallible truth of their own basic doctrines.

Not all religions are opposed to the investigations and findings of the natural and social sciences. Not all of them have at their core some kind of supernatural beings, domains, or destinies. Not all of them bemoan and deplore the ambiguities of nature and focus on the aim of deliverance into another supposedly perfect, purely spiritual realm or on the radical transformation of earth into some kind of peaceable kingdom stripped of all of its present ambiguities of predation, suffering, uncertainty, danger, ugliness, tragedy, and evil.

The concept of the secular contrasts with the concept of the religious, and if the latter is too narrowly characterized, then the conception of the former turns out to be too broad. It is devilishly difficult to find a characterization of religion that strikes the right balance between narrowness and breadth. And the problem of finding an adequate characterization of secularity is codependent on success or failure in resolving the difficulty of characterizing the nature of religion in a manner that includes its many different kinds of manifestation and exemplification without tending to make everything or everybody religious in some far too general sense of that term.

For example, secularity has long been identified by many in the West with atheism or denial of the existence of a personal God. Or it has been identified with the rejection of Christianity or of a particular version of Christianity. Or it has been identified with dismissal of anything ontologically spiritual or supernatural, as contrasted with all that is physical and natural. Or it has been identified, consciously or unconsciously, with rejection of some particular religious tradition or set of religious teachings. These notions of secularity are too provincial, Western, and restricted.

Alternatively, religion is identified by the influential twentieth-century philosophical theologian Paul Tillich with whatever gives ultimate purpose and meaning to life, with the accompanying contention that all persons are *necessarily religious* in the sense of being psychologically required to center their lives on and to live in accordance with a self-chosen, personally prescribed, particular type of ultimate purpose and meaning. I shall discuss Tillich's view of religion later in the chapter. But I can note here that his conception of religion is not only prescriptive rather than descriptive, reflecting his own particular form of religious faith. It is also far too broad. If it is impossible to be nonreligious even by deliberate conviction or choice, then not only does having a secular stance or outlook cease to be possible or to have significance. Religion itself then loses any kind of distinctive, appropriate, well-defined meaning.

Real religion speaks to the full range of human experience—from its darkest depths to its brightest possibilities. Its founders and great leaders exhibit comprehension of this full range in their lives and teachings. From their perspective at least, a shallow religion would be a travesty and contradiction. The genuinely religious sense of the sacred is therefore not of something sentimental, trivial, or easily attained but of something unspeakably demanding, transformative, and far-reaching. We see this with Moses and Jeremiah, for example, and with Jesus and Paul. It is inescapably evident in Mohammad and Al-Ghazzali, Laozi and Zhuang-Zhou, Buddha and Shankara, the current Dalai Lama and Mahatma Gandhi.

Today we may easily bandy about terms like *religious, sacred, spiritual*, and *awesome*, indiscriminately applying them to relatively shallow things. For example, "He plays poker religiously every Friday night." "My new car is my sacred possession." "Her face has a spiritual quality to it." "He is an awesome quarterback." But the embodiments of such terms or their correlates in the great religions of the world are of an entirely different order. When distinguishing the religious from the secular, therefore, we need to keep constantly in mind the warning to do justice to what religion means and has meant throughout the ages in its most haunting, challenging, momentous manifestations. Seen in this light, the sacred is not something to be trivialized or trifled with, nor is it something to be easily grasped or understood. Spiritual and awesome (or awe-inspiring) also need to be interpreted and understood in this context if we are to preserve their appropriate religious meanings. Something akin to the Confucian Rectification of Names is called for. Correspondingly, therefore, the search for a proper grasp of the meaning of the secular as set in contrast with the religious requires great caution and care.

In this chapter, I shall provide an outline of a conception of religion intended to fit this bill. At the heart of what is distinctively religious, I claim, is what Friedrich Schleiermacher calls "a sense and taste" for what he calls the *Infinite* (1958: 39) and for what I shall call the *sacred*. The sacred is infinite in the sense that it is believed religiously to lie at the heart of and pervade all things and to impart a sense of utmost seriousness, significance, and value to awareness and practice in respect to them. The nonsacred or secular, then, is encountering, approaching, or experiencing the world with no explicit attention to, acknowledgment of, or commitment to the religious sense of the world's underlying sacredness. Natural scientists, moralists, economists, novelists, or painters, for example, need not give principal or explicit attention to a sense of the sacred in their deliberations or executions in order to perform competently or even outstandingly in their tasks. Their pursuits can in this event be deemed secular rather than religious.

What is essential to the conception of secularity I propose is that it does not attend to the sacred or take the sacred explicitly into account in any particular contexts or circumstances. A person can be a secular person living a completely secular life when no sense of the sacred or conception of the sacred—in the distinctively religious senses of this term I shall develop later—figures prominently in any part of that person's contemplation, aspiration, or practice. In similar fashion, one can speak of such things as secular communities, secular institutions, secular governments, and secular pursuits in this manner. These do not focus on the religiously assumed or endorsed singular importance of the religious sense of the sacred. This sense simply does not fall within their purview. Profound intimation of the sacred as I shall describe it lies at the heart of all genuine religion, whether religion is monotheistic, polytheistic, mystical, nontheistic, meditative, or naturalistic in its particular forms.

I shall address these themes by discussing Tillich's conception of what he takes to be the narrower and larger aspects of religion, Schilbrack's analysis of definitions of religion, and the ontological commitment I hold to be common to all religion. The first and second topics will pave the way for my proposal of a way to properly distinguish between religion and secularity, showing not only what each is, but also what each is not. This is a large and difficult task, and I make no pretense of carrying it out with finality or to the point of complete satisfaction. But I shall strive to make a useful contribution to the necessary and ongoing task of attaining greater conceptual clarity in this important area of thought.

Tillich on the Narrower and Larger Concepts of Religion

Paul Tillich was one of the most influential theologians of the twentieth century. He gained special influence with his concept of religion, which he developed in many of his writings. In this section, I shall concentrate on one of those writings entitled *My Search for Absolutes*. In this book, Tillich claims to have found Absolutes in the realms of knowledge, morality, and art. He sees these Absolutes as pointers to or adumbrations of the Absolute of religious faith, which he conceives as the enabling, sustaining presence and power of Being-itself in all things.

Being-itself he conceives—following the lead of the German philosopher Martin Heidegger—as the ground of all beings and of all particular aspects of the world. He views Being-itself as the power that works against Non-being in its various existential threats in the lives of humans, imparting to them the ability to persist in their lives and to find purpose and meaning in their lives—purpose and meaning that enable them to press on with confidence and courage in the face of remorse about the past, uncertainty about the future, anxiety about the exercise of their personal freedom as unique persons, fear of fate and death, encounter with the ambiguities of the world, and other threats to self-affirmation they are bound to experience in their lives as finite and fallible beings. The fact that humans typically do continue to hope, strive, and live in the face of such formidable odds testifies for Tillich to the pervasive power of Being-itself continually upholding their lives.

He claims that the focus of religion, properly conceived, is not a personal God but the impersonal power and presence of Being-itself. The concept of a personal God is for him one sort of religious *symbol* that should be viewed as pointing beyond itself to Being-itself as the ground of all beings, including human beings in their daily lives, with all of the particular struggles, projects, and concerns of their lives. Nontheistic or polytheistic religions have their own traditions and symbolizations, and the whole complex of such varied religions and avowed religious outlooks comprises for Tillich *religion* in the narrower sense of the term. Rejection of all such explicitly religious traditions and outlooks, or the lack of focused attention to them in particular situations or endeavors, constitutes for him the meaning of the term *secular*. The contrast between religion and secularism makes sense, therefore, when each is *narrowly* conceived in this fashion.

But for Tillich, what he calls the *larger* sense of religion encompasses both religion and secularism when these two are narrowly conceived. This is because everything in human life testifies to and relies on the sustaining, courage-conferring power of Being-itself. Religion and secularism, taken together, represent for him "the Absolute beyond religion and non-religion" (1969: 131). In this larger sense of the concept of religion, *everything is ultimately religious* for Tillich. But of course this is only the case if the focus of religion, which Tillich conceives as the Absolute, the Ultimate, or the Infinite, is as he describes it, namely, the Heideggerian conception of Being-itself. His own particular religious outlook is thus intimately interwoven into his way of conceiving both religion and secularism. His is a prescriptive, not really a descriptive account of the nature of religion or religious faith. If accepted and endorsed, it makes everyone implicitly religious.

This conception of religion, if taken as a description of the nature of religion as a basic type of human outlook and endeavor, is much too broad. It makes the contrast between religion and secularism impossible to draw, given that all possible outlooks and practices are in the final analysis religious. Secularism as rejection of *particular kinds of avowed* religious traditions and outlooks, either in general or in specific circumstances, makes sense in this kind of analysis. But a secular faith that does not implicitly point ultimately to the religious Absolute as Tillich conceives it is not for him possible.

His particular theology lords it over secularism, whether secularists are aware of this fact and accepting of it or not. For all of its important insight and value, Tillich's "Being-itself as the ground of all beings" theology turns out to be not only too broad but also too question-begging and exclusionary. This kind of theology is well worth conceiving in its own right, and it has been and continues to be widely influential. But it is a particular theological perspective among others and needs to be recognized as such. It does not provide a satisfactory way of addressing the issue of the distinctive character of religion and its relations to secularism—at least not in the way sought for in this book. Its great virtue for our purposes, however, is that it exhibits the crucial importance in all religions, when properly so characterized, of having some kind of *ontological reference* at their core, which in Tillich's case is Being-itself. As we shall see in the next section, philosopher Kevin Schilbrack places strong emphasis on the necessity of giving careful attention to this aspect of religion in his interpretation of what an adequate description of religion requires.

Schilbrack's Analysis of Definitions of Religion

It is clear from Kevin Schilbrack's statement I quoted for the epigraph to this chapter that for him an adequate characterization of religion requires appropriate recognition of two principal aspects of religion that are essential to understanding religion's nature. Neglect of either one of them, he insists, would leave us with only a partial understanding of what religion shows itself to be in all of its historical manifestations. The first of these aspects is functional or pragmatic. It informs us of the sorts of things religion *does*, *performs*, or *promises to accomplish*. The second aspect tells us what religion is fundamentally *about*, what general kind of stated *ontology* or *conception of reality* is central to and the principal focus of its vision.

Schilbrack's search for an adequate characterization of religion, one that would allow for a meaningful and convincing contrast with secularism, is indicated in the title of his article on which I shall base the comments in this section: "What *Isn't* Religion?" If something has a determinate and intelligible character, it is important to understand not only *what it is*, but also *what it is not*. Religion is, among other things, what secularism is not as a basic stance—or what secularism is not in particular instances, types, or contexts of outlook and endeavor. And secularism is, among other things, what religion is not as a basic stance—or what religion is not in particular instances, types, or contexts of outlook and endeavor.

One can be religious without being a philosopher, for example, and one can be a philosopher without being religious. The former case is religious; the latter one is secular or nonreligious. Thus there can be religious or secular music, religious or secular architecture, religious or secular rituals, religious or secular moral codes, religious or secular political systems, religious or secular claims about and ways of living in the world, and so on. These differences can be ones of context and function, on the one hand, or of explicit ontological beliefs and commitments, on the other. Some types of music may give rest to the soul, thus having a function shared with religion, but not be explicitly religious. And religion will share in many if not most of the beliefs of secular persons but will be centered on ontological commitments that are not characteristic of secular outlooks.

Let's look in the remainder of this section at some of the functions typical of religious systems as Schilbrack describes them, and then at his proposal for the general kind of ontological commitment he associates with religion. I have no basic disagreement with his descriptions or examples of the former. But I shall take issue with his characterization of the latter. His analysis of the *functional* aspect of religion is appropriate and acceptable, I contend, but his description of its *ontological* aspect is unconvincing for reasons I shall bring to the fore. This conclusion leaves me with the task of searching in the third section of this chapter for a better understanding of religion's distinctive ontological focus and commitment.

Schilbrack distinguishes *pure functional* from *pure substantive* conceptions of religion and argues that an adequate conception requires an intersection of these two. A pure functional characterization of religion talks only of what practical benefits or assurances religion promises to individuals and societies, and of the specific sorts of these benefits that can be differently conceived. All of the promised benefits, he asserts, are ways of solving specific problems of life, such as problems relating to the body, to social relations, to nature, and to the uncertain future. Benefits relating to the body include, for example, the warding off of disease or bringing fertility to potential mothers. Those relating to social relations include initiating children into adulthood or providing rituals for marriage. In the category of nature, religious practices can be designed to bring rain or to ward off plagues. Religions also promise ways of dealing with the uncertain workings of fate and the threat of death.

We can speak of all such functions as *normative*, because they belong to the category of norms or values. Some religions, but not all, according to Schilbrack, prioritize such values and their roles in life, subordinating and ordering all of them in relation to some overarching value such as Tillich's ultimate concern or what is said to be of utmost importance or have the most comprehensive regulative scope in the living of an individual's life or in the policies and commitments of social institutions.

An important limitation of all such functional analyses of religion pointed out by Schilbrack is that some if not most or even all of the basic functions claimed for religion are shared with secular or nonreligious perspectives on the world. For example, physicians can deal with diseases and other problems relating to the body. Societies can be ordered along the lines of various kinds of secular belief and commitment. Agronomists and meteorologists can attend to problems relating to natural phenomena. And psychologists can counsel patients about daunting existential issues such as fate and death. It is also the case that secular approaches to the problems of individual and social life can have their own nonreligious conceptions of what is of greatest importance or what matters most in the living of one's life or of how best to prioritize the goals of social institutions. Functional approaches to the nature of religion are therefore by themselves insufficient to distinguish religion from secularism. This is one of Schilbrack's basic claims, and it is one with which I concur.

Schilbrack is right to criticize the pure functional analyses of religion on the ground that what is important for understanding religion is not only how it functions to *give promise* of solving vitally important human problems and addressing fundamental issues of life, but also the basis in reality on which religion provides assurance of its ability to *keep the promises* it makes to its adherents. The latter requires attention, he argues, to the substantive or ontological side of religion. An adequate conception of religion will *combine* the functional analysis with the ontological one. And the ontological one is religion's necessary concern with a distinctive kind of reality or aspect of reality.

Religion's focus, therefore, is not just on what will help or be of various kinds of practical benefit to humans, but also on how this help is assured by its reference to and grounding in some kind of specified religious reality. Schilbrack brands this blending of the functional and the ontological aspects of religion as "normative realism"—the norms being associated with the functional descriptions of religion, and the realism with its substantive descriptions (2013: 304).

How can this religious rootage in some sort of specified reality be generally characterized in a manner suitable for all types of religion? Schilbrack is correct, in my judgment, in stating that "this question is the linchpin of substantive definitions" of religion (306). And he is right to maintain that if this question cannot be given a plausible or convincing answer by a proposed definition or characterization of religion, it will fail. Schilbrack presents his answer to the ontological question by asserting that the realities on which religions focus are "non-empirical," that is, not directly accessible to the five senses. He claims that the functional norms or values essential to religion are nonempirical in this sense.

But then so are the norms or values emphasized in secular views of the world, as he readily contends and admits. So he further specifies that the distinctively religious norms and values are those claimed not to depend either on human agencies or on sources accessible to the five senses. These norms and values are held to be momentous *discoveries* or *disclosures* recounted by religious scriptures, teachers, and traditions—not ideas constructed or made up by human beings. The necessary functional and ontological preoccupation of all religion is summarized by Schilbrack as "normative paths based on superempirical realities" (313).

There are two troubling problems with Schilbrack's account of the ontological focus of religion. The first one is his use of the terms *empirical* and *superempirical*, and the second one is his insufficient attention to the palpable hand of human beings in the articulation and characterization of the ontological focus of religion, whatever that may turn out to be. In the first place, humans commonly claim to discover *values* in their relations to things made known to them by the five senses, and these discoveries should be recognized as empirical in their own right rather than somehow transcending or being superadded to sensible experiences.

And in the second place, it is humans' *experiences* in the world that have motivated and inspired their visions of realities that can give clarity and support to distinctively religious preoccupations, affirmations, and values. Even when divine revelations of the ontological reality central to religious forms of faith are claimed, such claims are made by humans in their relationships to the world and to their ongoing lives in the world. There are no such things as absolutely true or infallible revelations, because all putative revelations must be subjected to the tests of continuing human interpretations of their meanings and of their relevance to the quandaries, problems, and needs of human beings.

The purported revelations must measure up to the demands of many different kinds of experience if they are to impart assurance, support, and meaning to the whole of human life. Consequences of such ongoing empirical tests are always tentative, fallible, and ongoing—never absolutely determinative or complete. Human agency is always at work in the ontological claims of religion, despite the temptation of some religions or spokespersons for these religions to deny this fact. It is at least contributory in all cases. To deny the role of such agency in this regard cannot be a trait characterizing religion a whole.

Moreover, both facts and values are relational in all domains, religious or otherwise. That is, they exist in the relations of humans to various aspects of the experienced world. Neither would have distinctive, known characters independently of such relations. All of them, in order rightly to claim credibility or cogency, should have purchase in relevant kinds of human experience that at significant points relate to the whole range of human experiences, not just to those of the five senses. The five senses would have little of their significance for humans were they not intimately connected with the larger contexts of language, cognition, commitment, interpretation, feeling, and questioning that characterize human cultures and human lives. The term *empirical* cannot be confined to the five senses since their meanings depend crucially on these larger contexts and the assumptions, expectations, and interpretations these contexts bring necessarily to bear on every instance and on all aspects of sensate experience.

There would be neither facts nor values for human beings apart from such contexts. Both equally depend on *experience* in the larger sense of this term, a significance that is not reducible to or restricted to sensation. Values are thus not less empirical by their nature than are facts. Recognizing this to be the case exposes a serious deficiency in Schilbrack's conceptions of what he supposes to be *empirical*, on the one hand, and *superempirical*, on the other. This deficiency is a questionable feature of his account of the ontological aspect of religion. But his insistence on the importance of taking fully into account the substantive or ontological aspect of religion is a sound insight that is critical to understanding the distinctive nature of religion. Purely functional analyses of religion cannot carry the burden alone.

Religion and Ontology

In this section I shall concentrate on the ontological aspect of religion, because I think it to be the most promising basis for distinguishing religion from secularism. What general account of religion's ontological commitments can be offered that will do justice to its difference from those of secularism? The answer to this question relates essentially, I am convinced, to the ontological status of the *sacred* as that is religiously conceived and embraced. I shall provide a brief sketch of this ontology here and give it fuller articulation and development in chapter 7. Many if not most, or even all, of religion's *functions* can be shared, *mutatis mutandis*, by secular outlooks on the world, but not its particular *ontology*. Religion has a unique perspective on human life and the world with its claimed suffusive presence, power, and reality of *the sacred*, a perspective that is different in this crucial respect from secular outlooks. This is the basis of my understanding of the essential difference between religion and secularism.

What do I have in mind when I speak of the sacred and its basic ontological role in religious traditions and types of religious faith? I shall now offer a list of the traits I associate with the religious meaning of the sacred. A particular religion or religious tradition may not exhibit exactly all of the traits I associate with the concept of the sacred and with the ontological status of the sacred I claim to be central to and finally definitive of all religions. But a sufficient number of the listed traits are exhibited in the cases of these religions, I argue, to indicate that a close family resemblance conception of the sacred and of its crucial ontological status is fundamental to all of them.

The sacred as I conceive it, then, can be characterized as follows:

- radically set apart from all ordinary things and yet somehow immanent within each and every one of them;

- mysterious, partly ineffable, but experienceable;

- exemplary, whole, good, and pure;

- demanding to be regarded and approached with appropriate attitudes of wariness, deference, and seriousness;

- warning against being made common or profane, or being approached carelessly or indifferently;

- accessible, available, experienceable, welcoming, healing, and saving;

- eliciting incomparable responses of excitement, anticipation, wonder, and joy;

- contrasting radically with and set apart from all that is decadent, detrimental, and impure;
- inexhaustible as source of wisdom and depth of awareness and understanding;
- combining assurance of safety and deliverance with the call to wholehearted dedication and commitment;
- promising transformative power to meet the rigorous demands of this dedication and commitment;
- trustworthy, dependable, inviolable, reliable in all circumstances;
- imparting the courage to persevere in the face of all of life's sorrows, disappointments, regrets, sufferings, and dangers;
- lying at the heart of reality, immune to destruction, disappointment, or failure, persisting through all change;
- entitled to be the principal focus of human cares and concerns, commanding the utmost in respect, reverence, devotion, and awe.

A helpful short designation of the ontological status of the sacred as jointly described by these traits is given to us by Alfred North Whitehead: "a character permanently inherent in the nature of things," which he further describes as "a character of permanent rightness" (1926: 61). His term *rightness* is roughly equivalent in its meaning to what I intend to mean with my term *sacred*, as outlined above. It is an essential goodness implicit in the nature of things and inviting discovery and appropriation. It is a saving goodness of gentle persuasion and promise rather than of harsh imposition or threatening force.

This character of rightness is expressed in the Hindu term Rita (cosmic law, truth, or order) and in the Hindu-Buddhist term Dharma, the ontological significance and status of which are claimed by the latter two religious traditions to be similar to that of Rita. The Hindu *Isha Upanishad* declares of Brahman-Atman or the One that

> It moves. It moves not.
> It is far, and It is near.
> It is within all this.
> And It is outside of all of this.
> (Radhakrishnan and Moore 1957: 40)

This passage calls to mind my depiction of the sacred in my list of traits as "radically set apart from all ordinary things and yet somehow immanent within each and every one of them." It also alludes to the "ineffable, mysterious, indescribable, but experienceable" character of the sacred—a trait of it that I also list above. The tension between nearness and farness, as well as that between mysteriousness and knowability also typifies the Abrahamic faiths' conception of God.

The Buddhist notion of the *Buddha-nature* that resides in all creatures and perhaps even in all things also has a close association with my notion of the sacred. The Confucian *Mandate of Heaven* (or Heaven's Will) can also rightly be called sacred in the senses I have outlined, as can the *Way* of nature and its creatures revered in Daoism. The unspeakable and yet experiencable character of the Way (*Dao*) chimes in again with the ineffability and mysteriousness of the sacred.

This last-mentioned trait is also characteristic of the central Buddhist concept of Nirvana, as this statement of the Vietnamese Buddhist monk Thich Nhat Hanh makes clear:

> Nirvana means extinction, the extinction of all notions and concepts, including the concepts of birth, death, being, nonbeing, coming, and going. Nirvana is the ultimate dimension of life, a state of coolness, peace, and joy. It is not a state to be attained after death. You can touch nirvana right now by breathing, walking, and drinking your tea in mindfulness. (2016: 175)

Hanh's association of "coolness, peace, and joy" with Nirvana additionally calls to mind the "incomparable responses of excitement, anticipation, wonder, and joy" I included in my list of traits of the sacred.

The sacredness of the earth in the Abrahamic faiths derives from its creation by the God who in the first chapter of the Book of Genesis "saw everything that he had made, and behold, it was very good" (1:31). What eventually became the secular democratic idea of the inalienable right of all human beings to just and equitable treatment under the law reflects the theistic religious idea of every human being as sacred on account of being a creature of God subject to divine law and benefitting from divine love and protection.

The concept of sacredness is also reflected in the following statement of a Navajo woman named Nicole Horseherder in which she speaks of the "fundamental law" of her Black Mesa land in the Navajo Nation in a manner reminiscent of the Hindu concept of Rita—a land whose water supply is currently being usurped and polluted by a coal mining company. This law, she asserts,

> is given by creation and emphasizes how to live on the lands we were given, how to be stewards of the land, and how to live in balance with the environment. This law was established long before we got colonial law, long before settlers came to this land and established laws for us. We have to use it to guide us into the future—we should have been using it all along. It will provide clear guidelines on how companies should do business with us and sustainability practices they must follow. (2019: 22)

Horseherder's statement not only ties in with the various ideas I associated above with the sacred, but also with religious responses to the sacredness of earth, a sacredness that is widely ignored and severely threatened in the current ecological crisis discussed in the previous chapter.

In all these cases, we have explicit, fundamental religious references to a sacred presence, power, or law—an inviolable force for rightness and goodness—that is ultimately real and at the heart of the universe. This kind of ontological commitment is characteristic of religion, but is not typical of secular views of the world. Its endorsement and prioritization are definitive markers of the general character of religious traditions, outlooks, and commitments. Secular calls for urgent care for the well-being of the earth and its creatures may be grounded in scientific, prudential, moral, or aesthetic considerations. And it is certainly appropriate and good that they do so. But they do not turn on what I am claiming here to be a distinctly religious ontology.

Secular patterns, programs, and projects, and the promises they uphold for the lives of human beings and for their relations to the nonhuman world, may overlap in interesting and important ways with the benefits promised by religious systems. They can give fundamental purpose, orientation, direction, and meaning to human existence, for example, and they do so for countless persons, with their endeavors, hopes, and means of coping with the uncertainties and threats of life in the world that are grounded in various kinds of secular outlook and faith. But the functional overlaps of religion and secularism do not suffice to make the differences between the two inordinately difficult or even finally impossible to discern.

The functional roles of religion, important as they are, must be coupled with its necessary ontological commitments, commitments about the ultimate basis of reality that give assurance of religious faith's *ability to fulfill* its functional promises—a crucial point that Schilbrack rightly emphasizes. All religions tell us that there is a power of transformative goodness at work in the world and that this power is indestructible, can never be defeated by the powers of evil, is absolutely dependable, and must finally prevail. This power, I contend, can best be described as the assuring, demanding, empowering presence of the ontological sacred in its various forms of religious symbolization and depiction.

For example, the sacred may be seen as a God or Goddess; as a collection of gods and goddesses; as cosmic wisdom, mandate, or law; as manifested in a revered body of writings and teachings; as embodied in the lives of exemplary teachers; as associated with particular places; as an extraordinary kind of attainable insight and experience; or as resident in the depths of nature. In all such cases, there is attested access to the sacred dimension of reality itself. For innumerable people around the world and throughout their history, the sacred as the ontological focus of their faith is the ultimate ground of their hope. It is for them the central interest and concern of a whole way of life, explicitly acknowledged, experienced, felt, and practiced as such.

The hope of courage, renewal, and deliverance that the ontological sacred countenances and supports is what religion is finally about and what in the last analysis constitutes its definitive character. Philosopher and defender of theism Roger Scruton writes that "all of us, whatever our spiritual laxity, experience the constant need to refresh ourselves, to be purged of our transgressions, and to begin again with a clean slate. And this need for purity lies at the heart of the religious urge" (2012: 39). The longing for guidance, direction, purgation, and renewal of which he speaks, when informed and inspired by the presence and power of the intensely demanding but also graciously restorative sacred—as variously experienced, encountered, and conceived—is basic to all forms of religion. It unites the salvific function of religion with its ontological focus. This, in brief, is the concept of the essential nature of religious faith I am explicating and defending here.

Conclusion

I exposed in this chapter the error of assigning either too narrow or too broad a scope to religion, with a resulting distortion of the scope and character of secularism in its contrast with religion. I showed that Paul

Tillich's notion of the "larger" sense of religion is not really a description of the nature of religion but is rather an implicit prescription, that is, a covert expression of Tillich's own philosophical theology. This expression also has the consequence—unfortunate for my purposes here—of making everybody religious, no matter how much any individual may desire and choose not to be identified as such. Tillich's approach leaves religion with no determinate character that would allow it to be distinguished from secularism: a rejection of the fundamental project of this book. If everybody is religious, then religion is deprived of conceptual boundaries and stripped of descriptive meaning.

The search for this descriptive meaning is greatly aided by Kevin Schilbrack's indication of two aspects of religion that need to be taken into account: its functional and ontological aspects. He takes seriously the functional aspect, noting it needs to be properly recognized and understood if we are to do justice to the distinctive character of religion. But this functional aspect of religion is insufficient by itself and needs to be supplemented with its substantive or ontological aspect, partly on the ground that many of the functions associated with religion are also exemplified in secular approaches to the lives of humans in the world. A purely functional approach suffers, therefore, from the defect of allowing the description of religion to be too all-encompassing and broad. We also need, Schilbrack argues, to work toward an adequate general description of religion's ontological focus and commitment.

I endorsed Schilbrack's detection of these two essential sides to an adequate description of the nature of religion. He makes an important contribution to our understanding of religion by pointing them out and insisting on their joint critical relevance for this understanding. However, I took issue with his depiction and delineation of the ontological aspect. In its place I developed a different conception of the ontological side of religion, showing it to be rooted in *ardent commitment to the reality of the sacred* in the many particular ways the sacred may be religiously recognized, named, and conceived. I proceeded to set forth basic ideas associated with the sense of the sacred and to provide some brief illustrations of the ontological role of the sacred in various religious systems and religious outlooks.

I argued that the distinctively religious preoccupation with and commitment to the sacred—as foundational to the universe as a whole and as the supreme aim of human life—serve to make clear the essential difference between religion and secularism. Secularists may claim to hold many things sacred, even if not religiously sacred. But in doing so, they do not espouse but either ignore or explicitly reject the distinctively religious senses of this important concept laid out in this chapter. They do so especially, I argue, when it comes to the central religious conviction of the ontological character and status of the sacred I have sought to describe.

Chapter Seven

Reconciling the Sacred with the Secular

> Let it only be said that the world is shot through with a mystery that manifests itself no less in what is revealed by science—the universe of the galaxies and the eons, the eternally weaving DNA, the electrochemical flickering that is consciousness—than in the creations of novelists, poets, visual artists, and musicians. So we stumble forward, trying to avoid the dogmas of blind faith or scientism. We try to make ourselves worthy of a universe of which we are an infinitesimal part. We will not all agree on what worthiness consists of. For the religious naturalist, it is a mix of cautious skepticism and celebration.
>
> —Chet Raymo (2008: 126)

I have spoken so far in this book about distinguishing the sacred from the secular. And I argued in the previous chapter that religion, while sharing many of its practical functions with secular forms of faith, has an ontological focus that defines its distinctive character. This focus is what I call *the sacred* as religiously articulated and conceived, albeit in many different ways. I offered an analysis of what this religious meaning of the sacred finally comes down to in a list of its defining traits as I view them, along with some illustrations of how these traits are woven into religious systems and particular expressions of religious faith. To the extent that at least the bulk of these traits are the central ontological conviction and preoccupation of a form of faith, I argued, we can rightly term that form of faith religious and distinguish it from secular forms of faith.

The latter will typically have ontological assumptions and commitments different in critical ways from the distinctly religious sense of the presences, powers, and allurements of the sacred, although these secular ontologies may sometimes be more tacitly assumed than consciously articulated. And at times they may be secular renderings of what were formerly known as religious values and commitments. Secular ontologies are different from religious ones in that they do not focus explicitly on or may even explicitly reject the religiously understood and claimed ontology of the sacred. In this chapter, we will investigate religious and secular views of reality, earlier meanings of the term *secular*, the concept of the secular state, the need for religious and secular dialogue, and the virtue of humility.

Religious and Secular Views of Reality

Secularists may focus exclusively on human beings and their historical experiences, struggles, aspirations, and contributions. They may be principally concerned with searchings and findings of the natural or social sciences, the putative valuative realities discerned via moral or aesthetic sensibilities (especially the awesome aesthetic sense of the sublime), the technological accomplishments and possibilities of the present day, patriotism and love for one's country and its traditions and ideals, or just the practical needs, interests, problems, and concerns of everyday life. The implicit ontological commitments of these and other such secular pursuits are not always clear, but they differ from the direct and intentional focus of religion on the sacred and commitment to it as a pervasive and commanding reality.

In the cases where its ontological commitments are not clear, secular life will be preoccupied with such matters as accumulation of money and possessions, achievement of success and acclaim, gaining recognition and respect from others, dedication to one's career and the well-being of one's family, fidelity to one's friends, seeking political influence or office, working for social justice, pursuit of scientific truth, taking on in a practical way the task of being alert to and helping to ameliorate the current ecological despoliations of nature—but with no guiding sense of or commitment to the ontological reality of the sacred in any of these endeavors.

We should also not fail to take into account the secular outlook of nihilism—despair of any possible source of the meaning of life. Here no ontology or anything real, whether religious or otherwise, is of any help. We should also note that evil stratagems and alliances are not absent from some secular pursuits any more than they have been on the part of some avowed adherents of religion. Neither the professions and practices of secularity nor those of religion are immune to the seductions of evil. Claimed commitment—whether secular or religious—is one thing; actual practice is sometimes another. One can act against truth, humanity, country, society, family, colleagues, friends, or the well-being of nature, just as one can act against the teachings of one's religion.

This having been said, we should not draw the conclusion that the sacred is in all cases adamantly opposed to the secular or locked in mortal conflict with it. It is true that some Evangelical Christians in the United States have deplored as their principal enemy what they call "secular humanism,"[1] and that some secular-minded thinkers have for their part branded all forms of religion as obsolete, gullible, superstitious ways of thinking that should be summarily set aside as incompatible with modern—and especially scientific—ways of conceiving the world and the prospects of human life in the world.[2]

Viewed in these two ways, there can be no reconciliation between religious and secular forms of faith, and few if any areas of common concern that can benefit from their interactions with one another. I want in the rest of this chapter to take issue with this idea and to argue that, despite their important differences, many religious and secular approaches to contemporary problems and issues—to our collective human life in general as well as to our relations with other natural beings on earth—have much in common and much to contribute together toward progress and hope in dealing with these problems and issues. But before seeking to defend this case, I want to make a few observations about some earlier meanings of the term *secular*.

Earlier Meanings of the Term *Secular*

In this section I shall say something about the meaning of the term *secular* as that was long conceived in the Christian West. The original meaning of the Latin term *saeculum* is "generation," "age," or "extending over a long period of time." This meaning is alluded to in the New Testament Epistle to the Ephesians, which reads, "For we are not contending against flesh and blood, but against the principalities, against the world rulers of this present darkness, against the spiritual hosts of wickedness in the heavenly places" (6:12). The present "darkness" (*skótos*) is rendered as "age" (*aiōnos*) in a variant reading of the Greek text.

I remind the reader that "age" is the meaning of *saeculum* in Latin. In the New Testament period, the present *darkness* or present *age* refers to the world fallen into sin and ensnared by Satan because of the disobedience of Adam and Eve, as well as to the cultural and political domination of the

Jewish state and the newly constituted Christian communities by the Roman Empire. Meanwhile, first-century Christians (as well as the Jewish people of that time) anxiously anticipated the divine deliverance of the world at the approaching end of their present age.

Expectation of the coming new age of divine redemption is reflected in a later time by the counsels of perfection of Roman Catholic Christianity, namely, the vows of chastity, poverty, and obedience of those *regular* cloistered clergy who take monastic vows and seek to live as befits anticipation and exemplification of the redeemed world to come, in contrast with the *secular* priests who participate fully within and minister directly to the fallen world. The fallen world is, after all, the fundamentally good world that God has created, and it is seen as yearning for its promised redemption with the passing of every day, month, and year.

Thus originally, *secular* referred to a group of clergy whose ministry is in the world of the present age (*saeculum*), rather than in monastic withdrawal from the fallen world in anticipation of the new world to come. By a further trend of thought, this world comes to be known as the world of secular rather than specifically religious commitments, practices, and pursuits. But we should note that even here the secular is not absolutely distinguished from the sacred; it is believed to be encompassed within the sacred. I turn next to the concept of the secular state—a concept that helps us to gain more insight into how the religious and the secular can be mutually beneficial to one another.

Concept of the Secular State

Only later do *secular* and *religious* come to stand in sharp conceptual distinction from one another, largely as a result of the early modern Enlightenment thinkers' urgent need to find an alternative to their recent violent history of Roman Catholic and Protestant struggles to dominate religiously, politically, and culturally states, nations, and whole geographical regions. The *secular* alternative in this event becomes roughly similar to *neutral*, as far as religious matters are concerned. The *secular state* permits no establishment of any particular religious tradition but endeavors to grant equal scope to all religious institutions, beliefs, and practices, so long as these do not interfere with or seek to dominate one another, or to dictate public policies. The secular state has a suite of commonly accepted values and commitments at its basis and written into its own traditions and laws, and these are not explicitly determined by any particular religious tradition or institution. Seen in this manner, the term *secular*, as applied to a state, is a safeguard of freedom of organization, expression, and activity for religious and nonreligious citizens alike.

This freedom came to be seen by influential writers such as the seventeenth-century philosopher John Locke to be essential to genuine religious faith, on the ground that one cannot be *forced*, but must be personally *persuaded*, to have genuine religious convictions. In other words, it is logically and psychologically impossible to be *commanded* to have faith or to believe. One must be persuaded and cannot be compelled to do so. To think otherwise is to endorse dishonesty and hypocrisy and thus to be detrimental—not helpful—to authentic religious faith. This passage from Locke's *Letter Concerning Toleration* makes the point forcefully:

> The care of souls cannot belong to the civil magistrate, because his power consists only in outward force; but true and saving religion consists in the inward persuasion of the mind, without which nothing can be acceptable to God. And such is the nature of the understanding, that it cannot be compelled to the belief of anything by outward force. Confiscation of estate, imprisonment, torments, nothing of that nature can have any such efficacy as to make men change the inward judgement that they have framed of things. (1689: 7–8)

This passage and others like it in the *Letter* strongly influenced the founders of the United States of America, and its point is implicit in the First Amendment to the Federal Constitution.

The secular or religiously neutral state, therefore, is respectful of religion and does not stand in opposition to it. Its respect is reflected in its unwillingness to try to impose by coercion or law any particular form of religious faith, thus giving tacit assent to Locke's argument that an external compulsion of religious faith is not really possible and is, in fact, inimical to authentic religious faith of any kind. Thus, far from being the enemy of religion, legislation barring the establishment of religion is religion's true friend. *Secularism* in this sense of the term is not opposed to religion or the contradiction of it. It gives support to religion by being neutral with respect to its various forms of conviction and practice.

In light of these observations, the current cry by some people in the United States to restore their nation to its alleged former Christian character, and their claim that the Founding Fathers of the United States were orthodox God-fearing Christians who saw the newly formed country as a Christian nation, are highly debatable if not manifestly false—as I take them to be.[3] While it is true that Christianity—and especially Protestant Christianity—has long played a dominant cultural role in the United States as far as particular religious traditions go, its political role is firmly restricted by the First Amendment in principle, even if it is unfortunately not always strictly observed in practice. The United States in the present century is becoming much more pluralistic religiously than it was in the past, as well as having increasing numbers of its citizens indicate in polls that they are not members of any religious group or proponents of any particular religious persuasion. The secular state is a framework within which both religious and nonreligious outlooks, proponents, practices, and institutions are allowed to flourish. It is good that it be so.

It is also admirable and commendable for the secular state to admit to its shores or within its boundaries people of different kinds of religious and secular faiths, contributing from their various perspectives to the state's ever-changing and developing cultural resources. A healthy state in the present global world is a pluralistic state, not a culturally monolithic or backward looking one. Such a state admittedly has to struggle with new kinds of problems the more pluralistic it becomes, and these problems can certainly be formidable in many cases. But the problems can also be creative rather than inhibiting or destructive in their effects. Instead of being seen as dilutions or distortions of the state's former cultural character when nostalgically conceived, they need rather to be seen as potential enrichments of its evolving character as it faces toward the future.

The religiously neutral state in a rapidly changing global world is equipped to allow these enrichments to happen in ways that states with established religions are not. It should also be noted that state-established religions are no longer as politically dominant or powerful, especially in the West, as they once were. The neutral state is fertile ground for ever-emerging crucial consensus on vitally important political and cultural matters even in the midst of significant differences of outlook and conviction, whether religious or secular. This kind of state is a realistic basis for ongoing development of a commonality of civil commitments that can well up from the brew of cultural diversity.

Hope and endeavor for this end has long been the ideal of the United States, as inscribed in one of its most cherished mottos: *E pluribus unum*. Such unity with regard to central civil values can have both religious and secular sources, meaning that the two need not be viewed as necessarily opposed to one another. Instead, each can contribute from its own distinctive outlooks and perspectives the inspiration and motivation needed for adherence to common civic values. Religion and secularism can share many commitments and concerns even while having different reasons for doing so. They can intersect in many ways while diverging from one another in others.

As political theorist Cécile Laborde points out, "religious reasons are unsuitable to democratic deliberation" only if they "are intelligible exclusively by reference to the source of their authority—if they only appeal to a personal experience of revelation, or to extra-human sources of authority, neither of which is shared" (2017: 127). It is far from being the case that all reasons brought into the public arena by religious persons or institutions must be assumed to have a fixed, parochial, exclusively religious character. Religious citizens have much to bring to the table so long as they are careful to observe Laborde's essential conditions. Their analyses, arguments, and appeals can make use of the common coin of social and political discourse as expressions of their religious concerns for the common weal.

Before leaving this section, however, I want to take note of one example of how religion can also have an insidious covert effect on the secular state. It can do so when what were once explicitly religious ideas become entangled with the state's outlooks, policies, and practices in such subtle ways as to downplay or conceal their religious origins. What were originally distinctively religious convictions, commitments, and ideals now continue, in an assumed secular mode, to exert powerful influence on the state's vision of itself and its role in the world, and can do so in harmful rather than salutary ways. This kind of rapprochement between or unconscious intermingling of the formerly religious and the now avowedly secular must be brought out into the open and subjected to critical scrutiny.

An example of such unfortunate rapprochement is the idea, with a long history in the United States, that this nation is exceptional among the nations and peoples of the world and that it has the extraordinary mission of teaching, guiding, and, if need be, dominating and controlling these other nations and peoples for their own good. This idea has religious roots in such notions as America being the covenanted New Israel and shining City on the Hill with a light for all the nations, as having a divinely appointed Manifest Destiny, as having an exceptional status revealed in the American Great Awakening of the 1730s, with its postmillennial anticipation of the imminent return of Christ to earth, as needing to be faithful to its original white Anglo-Saxon, Protestant character—in short, as the United States being the God-sanctioned Redeemer of the other nations and peoples of the world. Religion scholar Michael Hogue has shown with illuminating detail in a recent book (2018: 22–53) that such ideas in secular guise have continued to exert unfortunate—and sometimes horrendously unjust—influences on the postures, policies, and practices—political, economic ecological, military, and otherwise—of the leaders and citizens of the United States from its earliest years to the present century.[4]

Need for Religious and Secular Dialogue

Paul Tillich famously defined faith as "the state of being grasped by an ultimate concern" (1969: 128). But in contrast with Tillich, I do not conceive of *all* acts of faith as being religious. And I do not think that ultimate concerns are restricted to religion. Finally, I do not think that ontological ultimacy is restricted to objects of religious faith. One can be ultimately concerned (in the sense of a psychological disposition) with any number of things. For example, it is plausible to think that Thomas Edison was ultimately concerned with technological inventions and patents. He spent long hours in his laboratory, with little time for sleep or for any interests other than these technological ones, while bringing such startling innovations as the incandescent lightbulb, the phonograph, and moving pictures into the world. His ultimate concern was arguably about science and technology, not religion. In fact, he was reportedly deeply skeptical about organized religion's beliefs despite his sometimes professed but admittedly vague belief in some kind of God.

In addition, there are other kinds of professed ontological ultimates than religious ones. Nature can be ultimate for scientists, for example, but not necessarily *religiously* ultimate. Physicists can argue that matter-energy is ultimate and lies at the heart of the universe without according to it any particular religious significance. Beauty, truth, or goodness can be seen as ultimates on which the universe rests by poets, philosophers, moral theorists, or other kinds of thinkers without giving to them an explicit religious significance. So even though theologians, philosophers, and scholars of religion often speak of religion as focused on some kind of religious "ultimate," it is not the *ultimacy* of a religious object—whether psychological or ontological—that is its most telling and essential religious character. Instead it is the *sacredness* ascribed to a religious ultimate, whatever that ultimate may turn out to be, that is the mark of its distinctively religious significance. Religions turn on *sacred ultimates*, not just on any type of ultimate.

There can therefore be interfaith dialogues of various kinds, including those between proponents of religious faith and those who are proponents of secular faiths, not because the former alone are oriented toward some kind of ultimate, either of the psychological or ontological kind, but because there can be a sharing of religious and secular commitments to ultimacy between the two parties. In such open-hearted dialogues there can be mutual respect for one another's convictions and commitments, and the expectation that mutual appreciation and learning can take place as the result of ongoing discussion.

Such dialogue is by no means easy, especially when deeply entrenched kinds of faith, whether religious or secular, are involved. When something seems too obviously true to be questioned on either side of the debate, special effort must be exerted to keep an open and receptive mind toward the other point of view. An assumed, previously unquestioned, and even unnoticed set of assumptions on respective sides of the dialogue must be brought out into the open for deeply probing, mutually beneficial investigation to take place. Philosopher Charles Taylor speaks of these entrenched assumptions as constituting "an underlying picture which is only partly consciously entertained but which controls the way people think, argue, infer, make sense of things" (2007: 557; see also 565). Until this assumptional understructure is exposed, it cannot be subjected to necessary critical examination, examination that can work to the considerable benefit of all participants in the dialogue. What before looked like intractable, nonnegotiable disagreement can now gain a focus on assumptions, formerly unconscious or hidden, that can be brought into the clear light of day and subjected to mutual discussion and assessment. Most importantly, the openness to questioning of these assumptions is now revealed and made possible, and their former seeming obviousness or indubitability exposed to critical scrutiny.

The starting point of all such meaningful debate is frank admission of human fallibility in all matters of conviction and belief, and the hope and resolve of expanding the range of one's beliefs by sharing them with the beliefs of others. Not everyone acknowledges or focuses on some kind of ontological sacredness, and those who do have this kind of focus may have much to learn from those who do not. Similarly, religious perspectives may provide important insights into matters of common concern for those lacking religious faith. Increased understanding and expanded awareness can be an outcome for both sides, and a posture of openness to opposing points of view can be greatly enhanced. Most importantly, effective cooperation in dealing with matters of mutual concern can be the outcome. Religious and nonreligious people are occupants of the same world and must learn how to live and work together in this world. They can do so with the convictions of their respective orientations to the world in the hope of exploring and finding mutual benefit from important intersections of those convictions.

Religious and secular outlooks on the world are admittedly different in many respects. These differences should not be underestimated or denied. But they can also overlap in multiple and sometimes surprising ways, and these overlaps—whether obvious or yet to be explored—should also not be underplayed or lost sight of. At least partial reconciliations of initially opposing points of view and attitudes toward life are possible when the partiality of all human claims to truth and understanding are admitted. It is not the case that "anything goes." Epistemological relativism must be rejected on the ground that it ignores the seriousness of different claims to truth and the serious consequences that can sometimes ensue from false or misleading claims.

But perhaps many more things "go" than we humans are typically prepared to admit. Ongoing interfaith and intrafaith dialogues among adherents of religious as well as secular types of faith can help to melt initial opposition to this fundamental truth. In an increasingly global world, continuing dialogues among religious people, among secular people, and between religious and secular people are not options. They are weighty responsibilities of our present age. Most importantly for our purposes here, setting religious faith in staunch and automatic opposition to secular faith—or vice versa—flies in the face of this increasingly urgent fact. Secular forms of faith can help to keep religious ones attuned to the concrete problems and concerns of the world and to significant developments of contemporary culture, and religious ones can help to attune secular forms of faith to the haunting mystery, majesty, and wonder of the world and of our lives in the world. These are complementary rather than oppositional goals.

The Virtue of Humility

Faith is usually associated with strong conviction, but we also need to recognize that authentic faith, whether religious or secular, is also often marked by profound humility and continuing openness to mystery. This essential trait of faith is captured concisely and beautifully by Chet Raymo, professor of physics emeritus at Stonehill College in North Easton, Massachusetts, in the epigraph to this chapter. Raymo was brought up as a Roman Catholic and earned his PhD in physics at the University of Notre Dame. He describes how he continues to love the rituals, sacraments, stories, and other symbols of the Roman Catholic Church and its traditions. He remains a kind of Catholic in his heart, but he no longer subscribes to the Church's principal doctrines, including its beliefs in such things as supernaturalism, a personal God, miracles as special interventions of God, or the prospect of personal immortality (2008: 17–21).

At a point in his life, Raymo became an enthusiastic proponent of religious naturalism, reassuringly discovering that, in the title of the book from which this chapter's epigraph is taken, "when God is gone, everything is holy." The absence of a personal God is by no means for him the eclipse of the sacred or of awesomely inspiring, significant, and sustaining religious faith. The natural sciences, and especially his field of physics, are as revelatory of profound religious meaning for him as anything in the Christian scriptures. The deepest truths of each field of thought complement the other, helping conjointly to clear a place within the forest of different specific religious and scientific claims where the light and warmth of the sacred can break through, unshadowed and unimpeded.

For the religious naturalist, the whole of nature, not a personal God, is the ontological seat of the sacred, and in Raymo's case it is nature as revealed through the natural sciences no less than in the creations of artists, as the present chapter's epigraph makes clear. His religious naturalism is a continual reminder to him that we humans are only infinitesimal parts of an incredibly vast and mysterious universe, a universe that for him—as indicated in his many passionately lyrical poetic books and other writings about the stupendous wonders of nature—is ineluctably sacred.

Religious naturalism is perhaps the religious outlook most receptive to secular outlooks on the world and closest to the intimations and commitments of deeply sensitive, open-minded secular people. Its intersections with secularism are many, and as Raymo reminds us, the secular explorations and pursuits of the natural sciences put us in touch with marvels and mysteries of the world that can evoke a profound religious sensibility—a feeling for and discernment of the presence of the sacred. But they can also warn us against dogmatism—whether scientific or religious—by making us cognizant of how tiny a part of the universe we humans are and how limited even our best efforts at comprehension of the universe are and will in all probability be fated forever to remain. This kind of awareness can be an avenue to the sacred, or it can simply be a route toward ever-deepening secular appreciation and understanding.

The awareness Raymo describes can conduce to humility and openness on either side of the two approaches to the mysteries of the world in which we humans are privileged to live. And it can allow for sympathetic, mutually enlightening discussions between them. The two worldviews may remain finally distinct, but the overlaps between them may also be greatly enlarged as each becomes increasingly aware of how much they have in common and how much more each must endeavor to comprehend, be faithfully committed to, and to aspire toward.

In chapter 5, we saw how the biologist Stuart Kauffman finds the sacred, or what he characterizes as a kind of immanental, impersonal "God," in the manifold, inexhaustible creative processes of nature, especially as these are being continually disclosed in his own field of the life sciences. Raymo and Kauffman are devoted scientists as well as ardent religious naturalists, showing how each area can contribute to the sensibilities of the other. The secular and the religious need not be opposed but can contribute to a far richer and more meaningful vision of the world and of our life as humans in the world than either is capable of providing by itself. I shall return to Raymo's religious naturalism in chapter 8.

We also saw in chapter 4 that for the Friedrich Schleiermacher of the book *Speeches on Religion*, the more we experience, feel, learn about, and celebrate our dependence on the immense world of nature, the closer we are brought to the reality of the sacred. For each of these thinkers and many more with a similar outlook, the sacred is present in every aspect of life and the world. It is not confined to some special, exclusive, nonnatural province or domain. With this outlook, the sacred and the secular are like the last two pieces of a complicated jigsaw puzzle, each complementing and fitting smoothly into the other and helping to bring the whole picture dramatically into view.

As the Roman Catholic priest of the Passionist order Thomas Berry proclaims, "The universe is the supreme manifestation of the sacred" (2009: 176). He makes this proclamation both from the perspective of his religious faith and from the perspective of his lifetime contemplation of and engagement with the wonders of nature. For him, the mundane or worldly is the sacred, and the sacred pervades the mundane or worldly. The secular and the sacred are woven seamlessly into one another.

We do not have to go far in our present culture to find deep opposition to this irenic view of the relationship of the secular and the sacred.

The proud, uncompromising scientism of the founding document of the Vienna Circle in the earlier part of the past century, with its rejection as meaningless anything that cannot, at least in principle, be scientifically accounted for and explained, is one example of this opposition, as are the fervent anti-religious writings of the renowned scientist Richard Dawkins. On the other side of the divide are those ultraconservative evangelical Christians who reject Darwinian evolution, the over four-billion-year age of the earth, and the nearly fourteen-billion-year age of the present universe adduced by present science. Their outlook is informed by unwavering belief in the special divine creation of all species of life, outright rejection of geological evidences of the hoary antiquity of the earth, and confident affirmation of the divine creation of the universe as a whole only a few thousand years ago. They think and act out of adherence to literal interpretations of the Bible that they regard as a compendium of divinely dictated and inspired infallible truths. They see these biblical truths as trumping any alternative claims to truth. From neither extreme side of this divide so established is there hope of reconciliation. In neither case is there indication of humility or willingness to consider a different point of view.

I shall not further discuss here the insistently anti-scientific, biblically literalist views of ultraconservative Christians. They may claim a focus on the sacred, but it is a cramped sacred, wholly walled off within the absolute authority of the Bible and restricted to an exclusivistic conception of Christianity and the Christian God as they conceive them. Such a religious outlook still deserves the name *religious*, given its professed recognition of and focus on the sacred or holy as ultimately resident in the hallowed presence and power of God. But the outlook rejects modern science, tolerance of religious perspectives other than its own, and anything approaching pluralistic receptivity to what can continue to be learned positively and religiously from the intricate tapestry of contemporary secular culture. Its opposition to the secular world is total and unyielding, meaning that it lies outside the scope of this book, and especially the concerns of this chapter. I am interested here in exploring the interrelations of the religious and the secular, not their supposed hard-and-fast opposition to one another.

The relentless scientism of the Vienna Circle's pronouncement, for its part, stands at the opposite secular extreme from most of what is important in a religious perspective, including the ontology of the sacred that constitutes, in my view, the basis of what it means to be religious. There is only ardent rejection, in this case, of everything religious. A similar rejection in the name of science can be found in Richard Dawkins's book *The God Delusion*. But in the latter there is at least some openness to the wonders of the natural world as disclosed by science that borders at times on at least a faint sense of the sacred.

The 1929 document, called in English translation "The Scientific Conception of the World: The Vienna Circle," announces the founding of the Circle, its mission, and its basic commitments.[5] Its mission is to "turn away from metaphysics and theology" (1929: 5). It endorses as meaningful and possibly true only those statements that can be subjected to rigorous logical and scientific analysis and, in the last analysis, "the simplest statements about the empirical given" (1929: 6). Religious statements, as examples of metaphysical or theological assertions, can have no cognitive meaning or truth value, and they should be viewed, at best, only as expressions of emotion or feeling akin to the evocative expressions of poetry and myth. A summary statement to this effect is the following:

> Neatness and clarity are striven for, and dark distances and unfathomable depths rejected. In science there are no "depths," there is surface everywhere: all experience forms a complex network, which cannot always be surveyed and, can often be grasped only in parts. Everything is accessible to man, and man is the measure of things. . . . The scientific world conception knows *no unsolvable riddle.* (1929: 5–6)

There is no room in this outlook for mystery, for possible realities lying beyond the reach of strict scientific description, analysis, and explanation. The epistemological and existential mystery that is an essential part of experience of the sacred is expunged in favor of only what can be precisely stated and verified by the evidence of the five senses. Nothing is potentially unknowable for science when its nature and capabilities are properly understood and employed.

The central and most important religious claims are banished to the outer darkness of the "metaphysical" (i.e., ontological) or "unscientific." There can be no truck with religion or the arts to the extent that these fields might lay claim to any kind of truth, as contrasted with mere emotional expressiveness. Moral values, to the extent that they cannot be submitted to rigorous scientific tests, also fall into this category. The kind of intense religious feeling (*Gefühl*) for the sacred that is given such great emphasis by Schleiermacher is stripped, as mere feeling, of any access to truth. The narrow outlook of the Vienna Circle is the secular *scientism* of which Raymo speaks, proclaimed with dogmatic, intolerant certainty. Its *scientific* dogmatism lies at the opposite extreme from the *religious* dogmatism of the ultraconservative Christians that I sketched earlier.

Just as scientism is a parody of science, so Richard Dawkins's view of religion as replaceable by science is generally a parody. There is indeed much in the history of religions, and especially in the Western religions that are his focus, that is violent, obfuscating, arrogant, ridiculous, and unsupportable. Dawkins does a good job of pointing this fact out in rich and well-illustrated detail in his book *The God Delusion*. But he overlooks all of the good things that religion has accomplished and continues to accomplish in the world, providing us only with a stilted, one-sided picture of its nature. He is oblivious to the intersections of science and religion at many points, especially in the more liberal, humble, open-minded forms of religious faith.

There is no recognition in his book of the kind of *religious naturalism* that is deeply indebted to science, eloquently set forth and defended in writings of Kauffman and Raymo, and at least adumbrated in Schleiermacher's pantheistic musings on religion. Moreover, Dawkins operates throughout *The God Delusion* with an unquestioning view of all faith as *blind trust* instead of possibly having the character and role of responsible, reflective, and reasonable confidence (2006: 208, 232, 347–48). Not all acts of faith fit into the former category, and not all acts of faith are religious. When we think of faith, we should think of religious and secular kinds of faith and explore their interrelations accordingly. For neither perspective is devoid of faith when faith is properly examined and understood (see Crosby 2011).

Dawkins's book, for all of its fascinating information—particularly about theories and findings in the biological sciences—and its provocative and entertaining style, does justice neither to religion in all of its forms, nor to faith in all of its types. He too, like the members of the Vienna Circle, is a defender of scientism, of the absorption of other fields of thought and experience into a final hegemonic rule and veto power of the natural sciences when it comes to questions of truth. Scientism, ironically enough, is one recognizable kind of absolutistic faith. Dawkins even subscribes to the Vienna Circle's conviction that there are no mysteries that are not ultimately and in principle amenable to scientific resolution, claiming that "we may eventually discover that there are no limits" to human understanding (2006: 420). The ultimate unfathomable mystery of the sacred is thus summarily set aside.

Neither religious fundamentalism nor secular scientism allows for rapprochement between religion and secularism. But within the broad array of options that extends between these two extreme boundaries, there is promising room for constructive dialogue, mutual insight, and helpful cooperation between adherents of the sacred and advocates of secular visions of the world.

Conclusion

Relations between the religious and the secular are more complex and varied than is commonly realized. There is the extreme view of the relations between the two that I brought under discussion and criticized in this chapter and throughout this book. On the one hand, for example, is the extreme idea that all reliable and empirically tested claims to truth lie solely within the province of the sciences, and especially the natural sciences. This is the secular view of scientism. On the other hand is the extreme idea that all claims to truth are subservient to the claims of religion, and where there is conflict between religious and secular claims about any issue, the religious claims must hold sway. This is the view of religious fundamentalism, absolutism, or exclusivism.

From the standpoint of this extremist view of the relations of the religious and the secular, there can be little sympathy or commonality between the two. They are locked in a no-holds-barred battle between two fundamentally different conceptions of truth and falsehood, value and meaning. This antagonistic picture of the relations of religion and secularity is what may first pop into our minds when we imagine their relationships. And as I have indicated here, there are in fact ardent proponents of either of the extremes.

Even though neither the religious nor the secular outlook on the world is hermetically sealed off from the other in the interpretation of them I defend, it is important to inquire into their differences as well as their interrelations. I have explained, developed, and defended the view that religion, while having many functions in common with secularism, has one determinate, all-important difference from it. This is religion's focus on the presumed ontological reality of the *sacred* with the traits I attributed to it in chapter 6. Secularism, for its part, usually has tacit or explicit ontological commitments of various sorts, but it lacks—either explicitly or implicitly—focus on the sacred as religiously conceived. I argued that there can be and demonstrably are ultimate concerns of many sorts in secular views of the world.

So it is not commitment to ultimacy per se that adequately characterizes religious as compared with secular forms of faith. What is distinctive to religion, in my view, is commitment to some version, expression, or manifestation of *ontologically ultimate sacredness* as I have described it. Specific types of this commitment vary from religious tradition to tradition, or from one personal form of religious faith to another. But underlying religion in general and suffusing its various modes of thought, aspiration, and practice is—in the view I have defended in this book—a compelling sense of the overarching ontological presence, power, value, allure, and demand of the sacred.

Only in the case of extreme kinds of religious fundamentalism, absolutism, or exclusivism is there a built-in, intractable hostility to the secular. For religious adherents of the less extreme kind, there is an instinctive positive openness to the secular because everything in the world is felt and believed to be pervaded by the sacred. Proponents of secular visions of the world may lack a sense of connection with the sacred and be secular in that crucial regard. Or they may expressly reject religion in all of its guises to the extent that religion turns critically on commitment to the ontological reality of the sacred. But the persuasion, conviction, and decision to be religious or secular in one's outlook toward and comportment within the world need not blind adherents of either option to what can be learned from the other one. The dialogical interfusions of the two perspectives can serve to broaden the outlooks of both as they wend their way in a world that is inescapably common to them both.

As we contemplate religious and secular views, we should be sure to take into account and continue to explore their many areas of actual and possible intersection. I have in mind a Venn diagram with the sacred circle on one side and the secular one on the other. The two circles are partially, but not completely, outside one another. There is also a vast area of intersection or overlap between the two, and each is impoverished if it fails to take fully into account this crucial fact.

Sacred and secular need not be in conflict. They can be friends. And their friendship can be and should be allowed and encouraged to be mutually enriching, enhancing, and even entrancing. Convictional openness, not dogmatic close-mindedness, can be the key to enrichment and growth on both sides of the divide. Neither should be regarded as separate from the other like an impossible bridge too far, especially not in our increasingly global situation. Continuing interfaith and intrafaith dialogical interactions, between and among today's adherents of religious and secular forms of faith, is an imperative duty, not a dispensable option.

I am arguing in this book that religion focuses explicitly on the sacred and that secularism does not. I also argued that for religion, the sacred has an ontological status that is of profound importance for the living of one's life, for relating to human and nonhuman others, and to the world. *But is there really such a thing as the sacred?*

Here is the poet Mary Oliver's affirmative prosaic response, or what I interpret to be her response, to this question:

> The wild waste spaces of the sea, and the pale dunes with one hawk hanging in the wind, they are for me the formal spaces that, in a liturgy, are taken up by prayer, song, sermon, silence, homily, scripture, the architecture of the church itself.
>
> And as with prayer, which is a dipping of oneself toward the light, there is a consequence of attentiveness to the grass itself, and the sky itself, and to the floating bird. I too leave the fret and enclosure of my own life. I too dip myself toward the immeasurable. (1999: 108)[6]

This dipping of oneself "toward the immeasurable" is what I am calling a recognition and orientation of one's life toward the sacred. It is what, in the final analysis—at least in my judgment—being religious comes down to.

To the extent, if any, that this sense of the sacred or something closely akin to it can be shared, even if sometimes only implicitly, by so-called religious and so-called secular persons alike, the distinction between them is attenuated, becomes less crucially important, and is no longer as divisive as it might once have been. Distinctions between sacred and secular outlooks are necessary because the two are admittedly not the same. But recognition of the sacred, whether the sacred is granted explicit ontological status or not, is perhaps a principal way in which the two stances can continue to aspire toward and seek to find significant common ground.

Acknowledging and finding ways to act appropriately toward the inviolable sacredness of *the earth* and all that is in it, living and nonliving—to cite one telling example—can provide much needed incentive for us humans to work together to protect and preserve our earth's health and well-being in our present age (*saeculum*) of relentlessly threatening ecological crisis.

Chapter Eight

Western Theism and Ontological Sacredness

> The conventional God existed outside space and time, a being beyond imagining, who lived in heaven, unaffected by the boundaries of human life. Thus, Western religion developed a language of what theologians call the *omnis*. God was omnipotent, omnipresent, all-powerful, in all places, and all-knowing. But the grounded God is a God in relationship with space and time as the love that connects and creates all things, known in and with the world.
>
> —Diana Butler Bass (2017: 25).

> Let me say clearly: All personal gods are idolatrous, especially any personal god we dignify with a capital. The great service to humanity of science has been to sweep the anthropomorphic gods away, or, at the very least, to show them for what they are, phantoms of the human brain. What we are given in their place is not Truth, but reliable empirical knowledge of the world, tentative and evolving. To be sure, science does not exhaust reality, or even begin to encompass the complexity of our interaction with the world. The religious naturalist seeks a language of spirituality that is consistent with the empirical way of knowing.
>
> —Chet Raymo (2008: 125)

Christian religious writer Diana Butler Bass takes note in her book *Grounded* of three "conversions" she has undergone in the course of her life and characterizes them as each "seeking a deeper awareness of God" (2017: 277). Physicist Chet Raymo, for his part, describes his journey of faith from an earlier Roman Catholic traditional monotheism to a deeply spiritual vision of the world and of our lives as humans in the world that sets aside a personal God in favor of a version of religious naturalism that places no faith in and has no need of a personal God. I discussed Raymo's outlook briefly in chapter 7 but shall return to it here.

I want in this concluding chapter to reflect on the similarities and differences between Bass's current outlook, on the one hand, and Raymo's on the other, and in doing so to free religion and the concept of the ontological sacred from its long-assumed *restriction* in the West to a focus on the traditional conception of God or to conceptions of God as such. I do not object to the claim that the idea of a personal God or some other idea of God is one important way of envisioning the sacred—and for millennia a profoundly influential one at that—but I shall identify religious naturalism as an alternative view of the ontological status of the sacred. This is a perspective that moves away even from Bass's third conversion that retains confident reference to some sort of God toward a perspective in which a theistic commitment is given up entirely and nature itself is seen as the focus of the sacred.

I embark on this discussion, not so much in the spirit of *advocating* religious naturalism as a spiritual worldview, although I have admittedly defended it in my writings on a number of occasions, but in order to *call attention to* religious naturalism as one significant way of broadening the conception of the ontological sacred to emphasize its central role in *all* forms of the religious life. Bass's third way of conceiving the nature of God is to my mind finally ill-defined, and in consequence it raises the question, *Why continue to refer to God?* Why not just focus on the sacredness of nature or on what in one place she calls "the numinous presence that animates the world, what Rudolf Otto called 'the Holy'" (279)? Her reference is to German theologian Rudolf Otto's trailblazing book *The Idea of the Holy* (1958; first published in 1917).

Holy and *sacred* are of course synonyms, and Bass moves tantalizingly close in her book to viewing nature itself as the sacred ultimate, so nearly so as to make me wonder why she has not at least frankly *considered* or even *undergone* a fourth conversion that would be content at last with commitment to a frank religious naturalism that no longer includes God, as has Chet Raymo. Such a response would point unequivocally toward this outlook as one of many different ways in which people in the West can keep brightly burning the flame of authentic, whole-hearted religious faith. Both Bass and Raymo have been deeply influenced by the Christian tradition, she by versions of Protestantism and he by Roman Catholicism. And both argue boldly for radical revision or what she calls a "sacred revolution" (Bass 2017: 26) of religious sensitivity, understanding, and conviction in the

West—she moving to the very brink of an avowed religious naturalism (as I interpret her thought in what follows) and he to an explicit endorsement and development of that form of religious faith.

Even though the term *God* is spread throughout Bass's book and continues to be given a prominent role in what she describes as her present thinking, the character of God as she now conceives it is never adequately or clearly explained or defined. She makes many suggestive gestures in her book toward such refinement, but never gathers them together in such a manner as to systematically articulate and defend her present conception of God. The term *God* has so many historically and presently misleading associations—at least as compared with what Bass describes as her present religious outlook—as to stand in pressing need of such clarifying attention and development. What she seems to assume or take for granted throughout her book about the character of God and the role of God needs to be brought into the clear light of day and subjected to concerted attention.

I want to note the three phases of Bass's religious development, or what she refers to as her three "conversions," and to show why I think her third one abuts the border of a possible *fourth* conversion in which the term *God* no longer figures and is no longer required. What I judge to be a troubling deficiency in Bass's otherwise wide-ranging, eloquently written, and splendidly evocative book could be in this way be avoided. Alternatively, she could have shown much more specifically and convincingly why the concept of God as she conceives it is still critical to her faith. In doing so, she could have given much needed greater clarity to the concept and to her present religious outlook.

She could have presented her understanding of the nature of God in such a manner as to show why in her view it amounts to more than fervent recognition and celebration of the sanctity of nature, important and meaningful as the latter patently is throughout the development of her book. Bass lays pervasive and heavy emphasis on the *locus* of God as being intimately in the world and spiritually present everywhere on earth but gives insufficient attention to the specific *character* of this intimate, ever-present, here-and-now God, as she conceives it. As a result, the distinction between a sacred God whose dwelling place is nature and an inherently sacred nature with no reference to or need for God is left unanalyzed. Is God for her simply another name for the sacredness of nature that she so persistently and persuasively calls attention to and rejoices in? If not, why not?

If God as Bass views God and nature, and nature as she views it, are not to be seen as one and the same, how should they be differentiated, and why is the difference between them important? Just where should the distinction between her radically immanental, this-worldly brand of theism, on the one hand, and a nontheistic religious naturalism, on the other, be drawn? An answer to this far-reaching question is never made explicit. To see why I believe this to be the case, I want to take note of Bass's three announced conversions, the third one as she describes it urgently raising the issue I have just sketched.

Discussion of this issue can serve as a fit way of concluding the present book by forcibly relating the idea of the ontological sacred to something different from the traditional Western conception of God—and even by moving in the general direction of what is today typically assumed to be *secularism*—but that nevertheless retains a strong and distinctively religious identity in its own right.

We need continually to remind ourselves that religion is not identical with monotheism, although it has long been assumed to be in the West, and that there is such a thing as a fervent religious naturalism that can boldly claim, with the title of Raymo's book in mind, that "when God is gone, everything is holy," meaning that nature apart from God can still be responded to with religious fealty, reverence, and respect as pervasively holy or sacred. Absence of God, in other words, need not be seen as entailing the absence of religion.

This fact stands in opposition to the following unguarded statement by Bass early in her book: "Religion is changing because its deepest questions, *those regarding the relationship between God and the world*, are being asked in new ways" (2017: 10; my italics). But she is a well-informed student of religions and knows well that not all religions, including the great world religions, are necessarily, primarily, or ultimately about a personal God or even about God as such. As I mentioned in chapter 5, Daoism, Theravada Buddhism, and Advaita Vedanta Hinduism are examples, as is the religious naturalism of Raymo and others.

Raymo's outlook and the outlook of those of like mind can go a long way toward helping to guard against misconception and miscommunication between proponents of religious and secular outlooks in today's world. Religion and secularism are not always as far apart as they are generally and unthinkingly assumed to be. The two are still distinct, but in many cases they may also have much in common. Their differences in those cases should not be allowed to elide or distract from their many similarities of outlook and conviction. Religion need not be seen as a bugaboo by those of a secular mind, nor need secularism be viewed in similar fashion by those of a religious persuasion.

From Radical Transcendence to Radical Immanence: Diana Bass's Journey of Faith

What, then, are the three fundamental "conversions" in the course of her life that Bass indicates? The first one is her conversion to evangelical Protestantism. She does not specifically describe the character of this Protestantism. But early in her book she speaks of traditional Christianity's commitment to a three-tiered universe, with God in heaven above, humans presently on earth, and the devil and his demons below, in hell. The directional orientation of this form of faith is *vertical*, and the worship of God is worship of a distinct personal, spiritual being who radically transcends the earth and whose domain is in heaven. A typical and prominent version of today's evangelical Protestantism is also oriented toward heaven as the place far up and beyond earth where those who are saved through faith in Jesus's redemptive suffering, death, and resurrection are privileged after their deaths to ascend.

Like God, the true home of humans as beings believed to be created in God's own image is not on earth but elsewhere, in the heavenly region of God and God's angels. And the ultimate goal of human beings is to go there. Earth is only a staging ground preparing persons for the final journey to paradise. But those without a saving faith in Christ are deprived of the hope of heaven and in consequence doomed to the agonies of hell. Three principal ingredients of this type of religious faith are thus its vertical orientations toward heaven and hell, a personal God of heaven who has created the earth and all its creatures, and the ardent hope on the part of humans to someday leave this earth and go to heaven—a place of limitless joy and everlasting flourishing in the presence of God.

The incarnation of God in human flesh, in the person of Jesus, is also believed to be a once-for-all, temporary event, not part of the nature of God. God graciously deigned to become enfleshed for a time on earth so that God's death on the cross could bring the hope of salvation to humankind. And that salvation is into a world radically different from this earthly one. Grace and love are parts of God's essential nature, but God's always being incarnate as an intimate part of the world is not. God belongs to another order of being, as do God's human creatures. This traditional kind of Christianity is other-worldly, not this-worldly in its fundamental character. It is ultimately about leaving the earth and going to heaven to be with God there when you die.

So something like this outlook and conviction was perhaps the faith Bass was inducted into by her first conversion. The second conversion, she tells us, was to "liberal Christianity as embodied in the Episcopal Church" (2017: 277). She does not give us more information than this. But this second stage led finally to the third one, in which she came to realize that she had viewed the world in her first two stages as "frightening, a place to be endured." She continues in this vein, saying,

> Although it took me some time to understand, I had largely wanted church to protect me from the world, a community offering the comforting arms of a benevolent Father in heaven, familiar rituals, a strengthening meal, and that promised eternal reward for being good. I had experienced both conservative and liberal forms of this church, but came to realize that they were different forms of a very similar thing, two versions of faith in the same vertical God. (277–78)

Her religious orientation had now shifted from a vertical, "up there" God and a remote heaven to the horizontal world as "the dwelling place of the divine." The earth was no longer a sinful place to be rescued from but a welcome home for the human spirit. And God was now "the love that enlivens the earth and the mystery that hovers just beyond sight" (278).

I appreciate and understand Bass's emphasis on the mystery of God that surpasses complete human understanding, and that, no matter how close to the earth God may be conceived to be, "God is still the One who hovers at the horizon" of our comprehension (121). But there must also be an at least partly intelligible conception of God to be surpassed. Bass gives us little help in understanding what the latter now is for her. We know that for her God dwells on earth and that God's love enlivens the earth, but we are given no further information about who or what God is or what God is like.

Is God a person? If so, how does God's distinctive personhood allow God to be pervasively present throughout earth and the universe, as she claims God to be? Has God created the world in which God dwells, or is that world coeval with God? Is the presence of God in the world just a pervasive sense of the sanctity of the world itself? In other words, how does God *differ from*, and how, precisely, does God *relate to* the world? Is God pure spirit, or does God have a material body? Is the salvation God provides confined to this life or does it extend beyond the grave? Is there a judgmental aspect to God's love, and how should that be understood?

I do not expect a full-fledged systematic theology in this one book by Bass, but at least some of these important questions could have been addressed if not only the locus but also the nature of the God of her third conversion had been given some careful attention.

Without such attention, any difference between her current religious perspective and religious naturalism remains unclear. Bass clearly believes that God is more than nature and suggests in one place the term *panentheism* as a way of labeling and describing her view of God and God's relation to the world. "Panentheism," she writes in one place, "recognizes the distinctions between things, at the same time that it affirms the indwelling force or spirit (typically called God) that draws all things into relationship with all other things. To put it simply, a panentheist says, 'God is not a tree; a tree is not God. But God is with the tree, and the tree is with God' (prepositions matter)" (39). But having alluded to panentheism in this way, she gives it no further explicit attention. Left hanging in the air is the nature of this "indwelling force or spirit (typically called God)" of which or whom she speaks.

In one place early in her book Bass acknowledges that "the problem of evil is real" but states that "it is not God's problem as much as it is ours" (15). There is truth in this assertion, but why is there so much natural predation, suffering, conflict, disease, disaster, and the like in a world inhabited by the spirit of God? And why does this divine spirit allow for, or what is its relation to, so much human-caused violence, cruelty, poverty, injustice, ecological devastation, and the like? Bass devotes only a paragraph to this serious and perplexing question about the nature of God as it relates to the pervasive presence of suffering and evil in the world.

Is the world God's body, inhabited by a kind of separate divine spirit or soul, analogous to the dualistic picture of humans famously set forth by the seventeenth-century philosopher René Descartes? If there were no world, would God still exist? Does God *choose* to inhabit the world, or does God *necessarily* do so? If the former is true, then God is clearly a personal being, distinct from the world and with conscious purpose and intent. If the latter is true, then God and the world are coeval, and God is a necessary part of the world. Which is Bass's view? At one place she speaks of "God's *intent* to dwell with all humankind" (171; my emphasis), implying a personal God or divine Being consciously choosing to do so, but she does not follow up this hint. We are provided with no sustained discussion of this issue concerning the nature of God raised by her statement. The latter view mentioned above is provocatively close to the idea of nature as inherently sacred, possessing in and of itself all or nearly all of the features that Bass attributes to God or to the intimate presence of God in nature.

Religious naturalism speaks of the sanctity of ordinary things in nature, while Bass's theism "listen[s] for the whisper of God everywhere" (284). Is this a difference that really makes a difference? If so, exactly how does it do so? Much of the answer to this question depends on what Bass has in mind when she employs the term *God*. But she nowhere clarifies or offers sustained discussion of her conception of God's nature. She talks throughout of God's intimate location or presence throughout the world, but not nearly enough about what or who is so located, and why for her this is the key to the world's sacredness.

She seems to assume much more than she subjects to sustained analysis or discussion regarding these critical questions. I suspect that she does so because she has a Christian audience mainly in mind, and thus that her references to God will be generally understood. But the God of her third conversion calls many of these assumed meanings into question, leaving unclear what kind of God it is to which she makes reference and also how and in what degree her current vision of the sacredness of nature differs from that of religious naturalism. I am not suggesting that Bass should have written a different book than the one she chose to write. I am only arguing that the vagueness of her many references to God leaves readers unsure of what she wishes them to understand about the nature of this "horizontal" God whose *consciously chosen* abode—if it is even that—is this universe and, particularly, this earth.

The Sacredness of Nature without God: Chet Raymo's Religious Naturalism

Chet Raymo has spent the bulk of his life teaching physics and writing books about his fascination with the world revealed to us by this critically important scientific discipline and by the natural sciences in general. He places heavy emphasis on the scientific method of reaching consensus through "quantitative observation, mathematical language, peer review, institutionalized doubt, and, of course, the willingness to say 'I don't know.'" To this list of the "tools" of science Raymo adds the principle of parsimony: "Never suppose a complex explanation when a simpler explanation will suffice" (2008: 52). "By ruthlessly paring away superfluous entities in our understanding of the world—including most dramatically, gods, miracles, and the supernatural—science has given us the modern world" (53). This emphasis on science as providing a method of arriving at reliable knowledge that can and should be applied in all areas of thought is reminiscent of John Dewey's similar emphasis, discussed in chapter 2.

Science has also given us a way to *reconceive* religion, Raymo argues, religion that focuses on the sacredness of nature itself and finds the truly inspiring and miraculous in the marvels of nature made known by contemporary science:

> With the discovery of the universe of the galaxies, the geological eons, the wonders of evolution, and the dance of the DNA, our eyes are opened to a majesty and a mystery of far greater dimension than the Olympian deities of our ancestors—or of the slightly more abstracted personal God worshipped by most believers today. (116)

Explanations based on extraordinary miracles; putative creations, actions, and purposes of an anthropomorphic God; or supposedly animate, human-like, supernatural presences or powers of any kind, actually explain nothing, Raymo contends (20, 32, 133–34). In particular, invoking divinity as a way of explaining something is the "most common cover for ignorance" (62). Science and its techniques of investigation and confirmation, on the other hand, show that "the smallest insect is more worthy of our astonishment than a thousand choirs of angels. The buzzing business of a single cell is more infused with eternity than any disembodied soul" (128). Raymo writes of "the numinous flame that burns in every atom, every flower, every grain of sand, every star—the hidden thing behind nature's veil" (20). In a manner reminiscent of the discussion in chapter 5 of Stuart Kauffman's encountering "God" in the universe's astronomical, geological, and biological creative processes, Raymo extols in equal measure "the signature of divinity in the extravagant wonders of the creation itself, not in supposed miracles or supposed exceptions to nature's laws." Prominent in these natural wonders is the miracle of biological emergence, evident in every living thing (114).

Paying careful attention to such things in all of their wonder and grandeur is for Raymo the religious naturalist's purest form of prayer

(18–19). He argues that science adds to, rather than subtracts from, our "our affective understanding," revealing in its findings "an apparently *inexhaustible* mystery, as layered as an infinite onion, that deserves at every level of knowledge our attention, reverence, thanksgiving, and praise" (40). Thus, we appreciatively feel the sacredness of nature in the depths of our being as that sacredness is brought to our affective attention with awesome power by scientific discoveries.

In such ways, science reveals a depth of sacredness and mystery deeply satisfying, enthralling, and moving, to the religious heart and mind. Absence of God for Raymo is far from implying absence of the ontological sacred throughout the world. The *secular* enterprise of science opens the way to a new *religious* vision of nature and of our lives as humans in nature—a new kind of rapprochement between the secular and the sacred, science and religion. While some religions of the past may have often promised us absolute knowledge, an absolute Being, and absolute convictional certainty, a scientifically informed religious outlook offers us inspiration and assurance in the face of the ultimate uncertainties and mysteries of our lives in the world. It reminds us of all that we as yet do not know and much that we never will know in full, but at the same time it propounds with a reliable level of confidence what is presently confirmed as probably true. It offers us reasonable and sustaining faith rather than outmoded religious rites, beliefs, explanations, and authorities of ancient and medieval times. According to Raymo, not even Christianity need be any longer dependent on literal adherence to any kinds of *otherworldly* myth (110). The supernatural is not required. The natural is more than enough. Science faces primarily toward the future, not the distant past. Religion should follow suit.

Raymo insists that "any religion worthy of humanity's future" should have three characteristics (114). It should in the first place be *ecumenical*, meaning "open and welcoming to [the] best and holiest of all religious traditions." His mention of the *holiest* of such religious traditions recalls the claim of the present book that the focus of all genuine religions, that is, what entitles them to the name *religion* in the truest and most enduring sense of that term, is on the ontological sacred or holy. In the second place, any future religion should be *ecological*, conferring unreserved respect, reverence, and love on the earth and all its creatures. In the third place, and here is Raymo's most persistent theme as stated in his own words, such a religion

> will embrace the scientific story of the world as the most *reliable* cosmology, not necessarily true but truer than the Neolithic

alternatives that presently give shape to the world's theologies. It will look for the signature of divinity in the extravagant wonder of the creation itself, not in supposed miracles or exceptions to nature's laws. (114)

In other words, and here is another way to state the third characteristic, a religion worthy of humankind's future will face boldly and unapologetically to the future and not allow itself to be stuck in obsolete, no longer credible outlooks, commitments, and convictions of the past.

Raymo announces early in his book his ardent commitment to this new form of religious faith when he announces,

> So this is my Credo. I am an atheist, if by God one means a transcendent Person who acts willfully within the creation. I am an agnostic in that I believe our knowledge of "what is" is partial and tentative—a tiny flickering flame in the overwhelming shadows of our ignorance. I am a pantheist in that I believe empirical knowledge of the sensate world is the surest revelation of whatever is worth being called divine. I am a Catholic by accident of birth. (22)

If we rethink ancient concepts in the ways Raymo urges us to do, then we will be equipped to recognize and respond to the sacred in all that lies around us in this world, a world whose wonders and mysteries are evident on every hand. It is these immanent, here-now wonders and mysteries—innumerable ones of them brought brightly to light by contemporary science—and not supposed supernatural presences or powers, that for Raymo command our devoted attention and thankful acknowledgment. For him, such attention and acknowledgment lie at the heart of inspiring and sustaining naturalistic faith. They constitute the essence of authentic piety and meaningful prayer.

Theism, Naturalism, and the Sacred

In this chapter we are looking at two religious approaches to the nature and status of the ontological sacred, claimed here and elsewhere in this book to be the distinctive common focus of religious faith. Diana Bass's Christian approach argues for a radical immanental conception of God, a God present in every aspect of the universe, the earth, and the living creatures of the earth, including the lives of human beings. The key to ontological sacredness for Bass is this intimate presence of God everywhere and everywhen. All things are made sacred or holy by a God who makes earth and other parts of the universe God's dwelling place.

Chet Raymo, on the other hand, agrees completely with Bass's insistence on the sacredness of every aspect of nature but does not associate this sacredness with the existence of a supernatural divine Being or view it as somehow dependent on the pervasive presence of such a Being. He rejects the existence of anything supernatural, such as the original creation of the universe or direct creation of the species of the earth's creatures (including the human species) by God, a supernatural heaven, or supernatural miracles of any kind. Everything sacred is through and through natural, and the sacredness of nature is brought into notably clear focus, among other ways, by the findings of contemporary science. There is no supernatural aspect or prospect for human beings; they are products of biological evolution just as are all of the other forms of life on earth. Nature is inherently sacred, not made so by God or on account of being indwelt by God—indwelt by the holy or sacred, yes, but not by a personal God.

I argued earlier that, despite the insistence Bass places on the presence of God as the ultimate source of the sacredness of the world and of our lives as humans in the world, she nowhere in her book gives the reader a clear picture of the nature of God as she views God. Here is a representative passage that suggests what I have in mind. Bass asserts that "the earth, us, home, and God are almost interchangeable characters in [the] . . . ancient record of humankind's aching search to dwell" or be truly at home on this earth. The story of our search to be truly at home on the earth and with an indwelling God, she remarks, "is a powerful story, rich in literary ambiguity" (2017: 170). But if "God" is "almost interchangeable" with us humans and every aspect of our earthly home, we are left with no distinct conception of God. God is mixed in confusingly with these other factors in a manner indicative of the vague treatment of God's nature in her book. We are told throughout the book where God is, namely, intimately with us here in the world, but not given much insight into what she has in mind concerning the nature of God.

Lacking such insight, it begins to sound as if Bass's view of the sacredness of the world is not that much different from Raymo's. What does a supernatural, personal, creator God—if God is that for her as it is in traditional Christianity, we are never quite sure—add to the picture Bass has in mind? It seems nebulous enough as presented (or not presented) so as to leave us with the impression that God is nothing more than a useful metaphor, alluding in its own fashion to the sacredness inherent in the whole of nature. But if God is supernatural, that is, separate from nature in God's ultimate character as pure spirit, then the idea of God being everywhere at home with us here on the wholly natural earth is blurred. God as a metaphorical flourish is different from God as a real Being. And the difference needs to be made explicit. Otherwise, Bass's theism and Raymo's naturalism look pretty much the same in all essential details. She does not intend it to be so, but it is unclear why it is not so. Her God has become so *radically incarnate* as to be indistinguishable from nature, or at least from a deeply sacred conception of nature like that of Chet Raymo.

An issue that neither Bass nor Raymo addresses concerns what in chapter 4 I called the troublesome *ambiguities* of the natural world. In a world indwelt by a loving God (Bass) or in one sacred to the core (Raymo), how can we account for, respond to, and cope with so much suffering, so much loss, so many natural disasters, such a precarious and uncertain life as we humans and other creatures have here on earth? This, surely, is a deeply disturbing matter of grave religious concern.

At one place in her book Bass notes, "The shift from God as the zenith of the great [vertical] chain of being toward God with us in a great web of belonging is the heart of today's spiritual revolution." She goes on to say that "God is not a far-off Weaver of the web, like the earlier Watch-maker God, who assembled creation and left it to run on its own. No, God is an integral part of the web, entangled here with us" (2017: 155). Her God is "the love that connects and creates all things" (25) but also a God that is somehow "entangled" in a web-like universe that here on earth also entangles both its creatures and God in strands of the web that involve enormous amounts of suffering, danger, uncertainty, devastation, and destruction.

If God has not woven the web and is somehow also tangled up within it, what precisely is God's role within the web and how does the web's existence relate to the existence, role, and character of God, especially given the web's glaring ambiguities? As we saw earlier, Bass does not view humans as predetermined puppets and asserts that their freedoms of choice and action have a lot to do with the cruelty, jealousy, jockeying for position and power, hatred, inequity, and injustice that has plagued human relationships throughout history and continues to do so to the present day. But what of earth's moral and spiritual ambiguities that cannot simply be attributed to evil human actions? What is the role of God in relation to these? Bass does not address this question, and as we saw earlier, this is a serious gap in her discussion.

Raymo also makes use of the metaphor of the web, as we can see from this comment he makes in the last two pages of his book: "Every object in the natural world bears within itself a mostly hidden relationship to every other object. In attending prayerfully to these webs of relationship we integrate ourselves more fully into the fabric of the universe. Grace, in this sense, is that which enables us to live gracefully" (2008: 141–42). But there is no personal God or pervasive, loving, divine spirit in Raymo's web, so his problem in dealing with its ambiguities is perhaps less pressing than Bass's. Still, he leaves us with the serious question of how the world's ambiguities are to be reconciled with the inherent sacredness of its every aspect, as Raymo conceives that sacredness. He does call our attention frequently to the mysteries of the world, mysteries that intrigue and baffle us but also inspire us and continue to motivate our ongoing inquiries. But he nowhere in this book inquires into this particular mystery.

In chapter 4 I did inquire into it. And I offered there an analysis of the ambiguities of nature that I think helps to show how they can be reconciled with robust religious faith. There can be no universe of any kind without natural laws. They give the order and regularity to nature necessary to life and freedom. Natural laws are bound sometimes to cause suffering and loss. They encompass the vast whole of nature, not just some particular part of nature—for example, humans or some specific group of humans.

The massively disruptive movements of tectonic plates have created the continents, islands, seas, and sea floors we take for granted today. Earthquakes and volcanic eruptions alter the earth, as do the movements of massive glaciers. It's not all about us or even primarily about us. Accidents are inevitable. The loss of some part of nature makes possible the gain of some other part. The evolutionary processes operative throughout the earth's history both create and destroy—there being no such thing as creation without destruction. A richly processive, endlessly creative world is an ambiguous world. Ongoing creation and the uncertainty of the future go hand in hand.

Death or loss of lives is the price paid for the presence of life, as the history of biological evolution on earth so clearly shows, the limited carrying capacity of earth requires, and the food chain dependent on the energy of the sun necessitates. The wondrous sacrality of nature is made possible in significant degree by its ambiguities. Sacredness and ambiguity go necessarily together in any conceivable world. Both Bass and Raymo could have provided us with this kind of account or some similar account. In view of the fact that religion has basically so much to do with how to live with assurance and hope in a precarious, threatening, and sometimes terrifying world, this kind of analysis would have strengthened both of their cases.

Neither Bass nor Raymo discusses a personal afterlife. We can be sure that Raymo is strongly disposed to reject it, given his thoroughgoing naturalism. Bass restricts her attention to her dream of a heaven on earth, with God acknowledged and revered as intimately at home with us here on earth. Her dream contains the hope for the continuing betterment of the earth, with growing concern for its well-being and for the just and equitable treatment of all of its creatures (2017: 269–70, 333). She endorses, in other words, a this-worldly heaven and makes no affirmative mention of some kind of life beyond the grave. So once again, her outlook and Raymo's are closely conjoined.

Conclusion

Several issues with relevance to religious and secular outlooks on the world have been raised in this chapter and elsewhere in this book. One of these is whether nature is inherently or derivatively sacred. Another is whether nature is the only reality or is there also another realm of the supernatural. A third issue is whether there is such a reality as God and, if so, what is the character of God, and what is God's relation to the earth and its creatures, including us humans?

A fourth issue is whether there is such a thing as an afterlife and how or to what extent this issue bears on the nature of religion itself. And the fifth issue is the relations of the sacred and the secular, a major theme of this book.

We have seen that nature is inherently sacred for Raymo. Its sacredness does not derive from or depend on anything other than itself, although it does point toward entrancing mysteries of the universe and our lives within it that are beyond our present or in all probability beyond our possible future comprehension as finite, fallible beings. In the case of Bass, there is also profuse celebration of the sacredness of the earth, a sacredness she holds to be evident even in such mundane things as its dirt, water, and atmosphere, to say nothing of its living beings, including humans. But she also seems strongly to suggest that the world is made sacred by the idea that God has chosen to be at home with us on earth and to become entangled with us in the web of life that encompasses the earth's diverse and innumerable life forms.

However, the character of this indwelling God is never made clear in Bass's analysis. For example, is God supernatural or natural? This question pertains to the second issue of whether there is anything supernatural in Bass's vision, including God, miracles, a supernatural afterlife, and so on. The answer to this question is unclear. Also in question here is the third issue of whether there is such a thing as God and, if so, what is the nature of this God. Is God a pure spirit or somehow essentially an embodied one? Is God a distinct personal Being or some kind of pervasive, nonpersonal presence and influence? In the absence of such explanations in Bass's book, the difference between her *theological* outlook and Raymo's resolutely *naturalistic* one remains tantalizingly unclear, despite the close similarity of their two views in many significant respects.

The fourth issue has to do with whether or not there is such a thing as the prospect of an afterlife for human beings. For Raymo, there is nothing supernatural, and there is no compelling reason to think that humans are destined for an unearthly afterlife any more than there is reason to expect such a future for any other kinds of natural animal. For Bass, all of the focus in her book is on this life and this earth, not on a life to come or on an unearthly, spiritual, perfect heaven in which human beings after their deaths might come to live. And she makes no mention of everlasting or temporal punishments in some type of hell. So with both Bass and Raymo we have firm answers to the question of whether genuine religious faith is separable from the hope of a life to come. The faith of these two authors is unquestionably genuine, and neither gives explicit credence to any kind of afterlife in some kind of eternal or everlasting heaven or hell, located in an order of being distinct from that of nature or from the mortal limits of life here on earth.

The fifth issue raised in this chapter as elsewhere in this book is the relationship between religion and secularism, or the sacred and the secular. Raymo's religious faith is profoundly influenced by the secular enterprise of contemporary science. And his vision of the sacred has nothing to do with the supernatural or with a supposed realm of being different from the natural realm we can experience and inquire into here and now. Bass's focus in her book is similarly on this world and this life, and seems to be deeply appreciative of the positive contributions of contemporary culture, including the enterprises of the secular sciences, to her worldview. Their intense preoccupation with and rejoicings in evidences of the sacred in the contemporary world show both Bass and Raymo to be keenly open to what can be learned from and affirmed in secular culture. They are not insensitive to palpable deficiencies in this culture or to its frequent profanations of the ontological sacred, but they do not reject it out of hand. Secularism deserves warranted criticism, but also appropriate praise. If I may be permitted to return to my image in the previous chapter of the Venn diagram, the intersection of the sacred and the secular circles is considerably widened by the visions of these two thinkers, and what might have been thought of as a vast and even unbridgeable difference between them is greatly reduced. There is much in common between the sacred and secular outlooks that await ongoing exploration and discovery, much that each can learn from the other, and great need for dialogues between them to be continuously encouraged, broadened, and intensified.

Notes

Chapter Three

1. For sustained discussion of and insistence on this point, see Hossenfelder 2018. A German quantum physicist, Hossenfelder warns against allowing the seductive beauty and elegance of mathematically formulated scientific theories to lure scientists into believing that the theories have no essential need of *empirical* confirmation or disconfirmation in order to be accepted as true. She sees a strong tendency in this direction in the attitudes and practices of a number of theoretical physicists of recent times.

2. See Crosby 2018b for extensive defense of the claim that responsible and defensible faith, whether religious or secular, is involved in a never-ending process of critical examination and testing. It is processive rather than static. This means that doubting and questioning are not inimical to genuine faith but essential to it. Existential conviction plays an essential role in the nature of faith, but so does ongoing critical analysis, not only of the intellectual contents of faith but also of the continuing adequacy of its underlying convictional stance. The latter is always in need of exposure to the critical tests of continuing thought, experience, and practice, both individually and in community with others. There is unavoidable risk in any stance of faith, and this risk must be frankly acknowledged, accepted, and faced up to. Supposed immunity to questioning or any degree of doubt or unease is the sign of a dead and insincere faith, not an active and honest one.

Chapter Five

1. See Antal's book (2018: 57), where he mentions "salvation in this world and in the next" as important Christian concerns.

2. www.ecodharma.com.

3. For examination of the nature of faith as well as for the argument that faith plays a fundamental role in all reasoning just as reasoning plays a fundamental

role in all responsible acts of faith, see Crosby 2011. Thus "faith communities" or "people of faith" necessarily include secular as well as religious reasoners—despite the prevalent tendency to restrict the two labels only to religious communities or religious persons.

Chapter Seven

1. A good example of this attitude toward all things secular is the outlook of the Evangelical Christian theologian Francis Schaeffer. A discussion of Schaeffer's views that displays his total opposition to what he calls *secular humanism* is contained in FitzGerald 2017 (348–63). See also Schaeffer 1982.

2. Biologist Richard Dawkins is an influential advocate of dismissing out of hand theistic religion, and by implication all religion, in the name of science. See his 2006 book *The God Delusion*. The logical positivists of the Vienna Circle took a similar stance. I'll have more to say about both Dawkins's book and the Vienna Circle later in the chapter.

3. A balanced critical discussion of the claim that the United States was founded as a Christian rather than secular nation is provided by John Fea's book *Was America Founded as a Christian Nation?* (2016).

4. For discussion of some ways in which religions can be formidable forces for evil as well as good in the world, see Crosby 2018a. Human history continually warns us against the illusion that religious influences have always been or ever will be unquestionably helpful or benign. Religions are as subject to distortion, corruption, and misuse as is any other kind of human interest or pursuit, and their potential for demonic injustice and evil should never be underestimated. Hence, not all rapprochements of the allegedly sacred and the secular should be sought for or desired.

5. My wife Pam located this document. We read and discussed it together on several occasions.

6. I thank my good friend Tom Clark for bringing this passage to my attention. Mary Oliver's poetry is for me a continual, many-sided evocation of the sacred, an evocation that is for her as well as for me an essential part of a purposeful, meaningful life. One does not have to be a participant in a religious institution or tied to a particular religious tradition to have this sense as a central part of one's life, although it does help to celebrate it in a community of like-minded people, each striving in various ways to refresh and strengthen this vital sensibility in one another.

Works Cited

Antal, Jim. 2018. *Climate Church, Climate World: How People of Faith Must Work for Change.* Lanham, MD: Rowman and Littlefield.
Baier, Kurt. 1969. *The Moral Point of View: A Rational Basis of Ethics.* Ithaca, NY: Cornell University Press.
Bamberger, Bernard J. 1964. *The Story of Judaism.* New York: Schocken.
Bass, Diana Butler. 2017. *Grounded: Finding God in the World; A Spiritual Revolution.* New York: HarperOne.
Berry, Thomas. 2009. *The Sacred Universe: Earth, Spirituality, and Religion in the Twenty-First Century.* Edited by Mary Evelyn Tucker. New York: Columbia University Press.
Bodhi, Bhikkhu, ed. 2005. *In the Buddha's Words: An Anthology of Discourses from the Pāli Canon.* Somerville, MA: Wisdom.
Borel, Brooke. 2019. "How Professional Truth Seekers Search for Answers." *Scientific American*, September.
Borg, Marcus J., and John Dominic Crossan. 2009. *The First Christmas: What the Gospels Really Teach about Jesus's Birth.* New York: HarperOne.
Crosby, Donald A. 2008. *Living with Ambiguity: Religious Naturalism and the Menace of Evil.* Albany: State University of New York Press.
———. 2011. *Faith and Reason: Their Roles in Religious and Secular Life.* Albany: State University of New York Press.
———. 2018a. "The Abrahamic Faiths as Forces for Good or Evil." *American Journal of Theology and Philosophy* 39, no. 3 (September): 29–47.
———. 2018b. *Faith and Freedom: Contexts, Choices, and Crises in Religious Commitments.* London: Routledge.
———. 2020. *Primordial Time: Its Irreducible Reality, Human Significance, and Ecological Import.* Lanham, MD: Lexington Books.
Darwin, Charles. n.d. *The Origin of Species by Means of Natural Selection; or, The Preservation of Favored Races in the Struggle for Life,* and *The Descent of Man and Selection in Relation to Sex.* New York: Modern Library.

Dawkins, Richard. 2006. *The God Delusion*. New York: Houghton Mifflin.
Dewey, John. 1960. *The Quest for Certainty: A Study of the Relation of Knowledge and Action*. New York: Capricorn.
Epstein, Isidore. 1964. *Judaism: A Historical Presentation*. Baltimore: Penguin.
Fea, John. 2016. *Was America Founded as a Christian Nation?* Rev. ed. Louisville, KY: Westminster John Knox Press.
FitzGerald, Frances. 2017. *The Evangelicals: The Struggle to Shape America*. New York: Simon and Schuster.
Frankl, Viktor E. 2006. *Man's Search for Meaning*. Translated by Ilse Lasch. Boston: Beacon.
Hägglund, Martin. 2019. *This Life: Secular Faith and Spiritual Freedom*. New York: Pantheon.
Hanh, Hans, Otto Neurath, and Rudolph Carnap. "Scientific Conception of the World: The Vienna Circle." 1929. http://citeseerx.ist.psu.edu/viewdoc/download?doi=10.1.1.477.4758&rep=rep1&type=pdf.
Hanh, Thich Nhat. 2016. *At Home in the World: Stories and Essential Teachings from a Monk's Life*. London: Rider.
Hogue, Michael S. 2018. *American Immanence: Democracy for an Uncertain World*. New York: Columbia University Press.
The Holy Scriptures according to the Masoretic Text. 1952. Philadelphia: Jewish Publication Society of America.
Horseherder, Nicole. 2019. "Beautiful Water Speaks." *Sierra*, November/December, 22–23.
Hossenfelder, Sabine. 2018. *Lost in Math: How Beauty Leads Physics Astray*. New York: Basic Books.
James, William. 1977. "The Moral Philosopher and the Moral Life." In *The Writings of William James: A Comprehensive Edition*, edited by John J. McDermott, 610–29. Chicago: University of Chicago Press.
Jenkins, Philip. 2017. *Crucible of Faith: The Ancient Revolution That Made Our Modern Religious World*. New York: Basic Books.
Johnson, Brad. 2012. "Inhofe: God Says Global Warming Is a Hoax." ThinkProgress, March 9. https://archive.thinkprogress.org/inhofe-god-says-global-warming-is-a-hoax-cf1acaeb77c3/.
Kant, Immanuel. 1960. *Religion within the Limits of Reason Alone*. Translated by Theodore M. Greene and Hoyt H. Hudson. New York: Harper Torchbooks.
Kauffman, Stuart A. 2008. *Reinventing the Sacred: A New View of Science, Reason, and Religion*. New York: Basic Books.
Laborde, Cécile. 2017. *Liberalism's Religion*. Cambridge, MA: Harvard University Press.
Locke, John. 1689. *A Letter Concerning Toleration*. Translated by William Popple. https://socialsciences.mcmaster.ca/econ/ugcm/3ll3/locke/toleration.pdf.
Meland, Bernard Eugene. 1966. *The Secularization of Modern Cultures*. New York: Oxford University Press.

Natarajan, Priyamvada. 2019. "In Search of Planet X." *New York Review of Books*, October 24, 39–41.
Oliver, Mary. 1999. *Winter Hours: Prose, Prose Poems, and Poems*. New York: Mariner.
Otto, Rudolf. 1958. *The Idea of the Holy: An Inquiry into the Non-rational Factor in the Idea of the Divine and Its Relation to the Rational*. Translated by John W. Harvey. New York: Oxford University Press.
Pelikan, Jaroslav. 1984. *The Christian Tradition: A History of the Development of Doctrine*. Vol. 4, *Reformation of Church and Dogma (1300–1700)*. Chicago: University of Chicago Press.
The Qur'an. 2015. Translated by M. A. S. Abdel Haleem. New York: Oxford University Press.
Radhakrishnan, Sarvepalli, and Charles A. Moore, eds. 1971. *A Sourcebook in Indian Philosophy*. Princeton, NJ: Princeton University Press.
Raymo, Chet. 2008. *When God Is Gone Everything Is Holy: The Making of a Religious Naturalist*. Notre Dame, IN: Sorin.
Rushdoony, Rousas John. 1995. *By What Standard: An Analysis of the Philosophy of Cornelius Van Til*. Vallecito, CA: Ross House Books.
Schaeffer, Francis A. 1982. *The Complete Works of Francis A. Schaeffer: A Christian World View*. Vol. 5, *A Christian View of the West*. Wheaton, IL: Crossway.
———. 2005. *How Should We Then Live? The Rise and Decline of Western Thought and Culture*. L'Abri 50th anniversary ed. Wheaton, IL: Crossway.
Schilbrack, Kevin. 2013. "What *Isn't* Religion?" *Journal of Religion* 93, no. 3 (July): 291–319.
Schleiermacher, Friedrich. 1958. *On Religion: Speeches to Its Cultured Despisers*. Translated by John Oman. New York: Harper.
Scruton, Roger. 2012. *The Face of God: The Gifford Lectures*. London: Bloomsbury Academic.
Spinoza, Benedict de. 1955. *The Ethics*. In *The Chief Works of Benedict de Spinoza*, translated by R. H. M. Elwes, 2:45–271. New York: Dover.
Tauber, Alfred I. 2009. *Science and the Quest for Meaning*. Waco, TX: Baylor University Press.
Taylor, Barbara Brown. 2019. *Holy Envy: Finding God in the Faith of Others*. New York: HarperOne.
Taylor, Charles. 2007. *A Secular Age*. Cambridge, MA: Harvard University Press.
Tillich, Paul. 1969. *My Search for Absolutes*. New York: Simon and Schuster.
Waley, Arthur, ed. 1958. *The Way and Its Power: Lao Tzu's Tao Tê Ching and Its Place in Chinese Thought*. New York: Grove.
Whitehead, Alfred North. 1926. *Religion in the Making*. New York: Macmillan.
———. 1958. *Modes of Thought*. New York: Capricorn.
———. 1967. *Adventures of Ideas*. New York: Free Press.
Wilson, Edward O., 2016. "The Global Solution to Extinction" *New York Times*, March 12, sec. SR, p. 7.

Wohlleben, Peter. 2017. *The Hidden Life of Trees: What They Feel, How They Communicate*. Translated by Jane Billinghurst. Vancouver: Greystone.

Wu, Kuang-ming. 1990. *The Butterfly as Companion: Meditations on the First Three Chapters of the Chuang Tzu*. Albany: State University of New York Press.

Index

Advaita Vedanta Hinduism, 105
Aesthetic experiences, roles of beauty and ugliness in, 112–13. *See also* Ecological crisis, aesthetic responses to
Antal, Jim, 102–103, 171n1
Arkani-Hamed, Nima, 73
Augustine, 23

Baier, Kurt, 10, 111
Bamberger, Bernard J., 41
Bass, Diana Butler, 14–15; concept of God ill-defined by, 154–55, 158–60, 164–66, 168; defends sacredness of nature, 163–64; does not address ambiguities of the natural world, 165–66; does not envision an afterlife, 167, 168; endorses panentheism but does not analyze it in any depth, 159; her journey of faith, 157–60; moves tantalizingly close to religious naturalism, 154–56, 159, 165; profoundly open to what can be learned from and affirmed in secular culture, 168–69; sees God as entangled with everything else in a great web of nature, 165
Berry, Thomas, 146

Bible, Christian, claimed original autographs of, 41
Bible, Hebrew, infallibility of defended by Akiba, 41; "oral Torah" as necessary supplement to defended by Hillel and R. Ishmael 41; Pharisees' and Sadducees' different interpretations of, 41–42; and sacredness of nature, 107
Biblical Criticism, 40
Borg, Marcus and Crossan, John Dominic, their emphasis on Christianity as focused on transforming this temporal world, not just on the hope of an afterlife, 28–29
Brahman-Atman, 128
Buddha-Nature, 129
Buddhism, codependent origination in, 104; concept of Emptiness in, 104; concept of Nirvana in, 129; and Indra's Net, 104; relations to ecological crisis, 104; Theravada, 75–76, 105
Buddhist Eco-Dharma Centre, 104

Christians, opposition to religious pluralism and secular culture

Christians *(continued)*
  total and unyielding, 147;
  ultraconservative, 147
Cells, biological, analogy to relations of sacred and secular, 1, 2, 3, 7
Certainty, existential, not same as epistemic certainty, 75
Clark, Tom, 172n6
Complementary relations of sacred and secular, 1–3, 7–8, 11
Constable, John, 113
Crosby, Pamela, 31, 172n5
Crossan, John Dominic. *See* Borg, Marcus

Dante, Alighieri, 113
Daoism, 9, 90–93, 105; living in harmony with nature the central ideal of, 92; the sacred texts of seen as human productions and as metaphorical, evocative, playful, and poetic rather than literal or doctrinal, 92–93; nature the religious ultimate of, 91–92; no dream of personal immortality in, 92; sacred texts as inviting personal self-discovery, 93
Darwin, Charles, 81, 82, 87
Dawkins, Richard, 14, 147–48; advocate of scientism, 149; does no justice to the character of religion in all of its forms, 149; rejects theism, and by implication all religion, out of hand, 172n2; sees faith erroneously as blind trust, 149; sees no mysteries beyond the reach of science, 149
Descartes, René, 43–44, 159
Dewey, John, 7–8, 35, 60–61, 71–72, 73, 74, 75, 77–78
Dialogue, admission of human fallibility essential to, 143; convictional openness the key to, 151; no essential barriers to between religious and secular forms of faith, 149–50; ongoing importance and need for among proponents of religious and secular faiths, 13–14, 54, 142–44, 169; religious and secular opponents of, 14; values of, 143–44

E pluribus unum, 12, 140–41
Ecological crisis, 8, 10–11, 102–10; aesthetic responses to, 112–14; a Buddhist response to, 104; a common cause for secular and sacred responses, 114–15; a monotheistic response to, 102–104; moral responses to, 110–12; peremptory dismissal of by James Inhofe, 103; prudential responses to, 109–10; scientific responses to, 104–109; secular responses to, 109–14; symptoms of, 109–10
Edison, Thomas, 142
Einstein, Albert, 44
Everlasting afterlife, sets up dualistic hiatus between humans and rest of nature, 30; meaning of life not dependent on, 30–31; temptation to endless delay of work needing to be done in, 29–30; undesirability and implausibility of, 30–31
Evil, seductions of in religious and secular life, 136–37

Faith, doubt not inimical to but essential for active and honest faith, 171n2; can have secular or religious forms 17, 171–72n3; needs to be reasonable rather than blind, 86, 171–72n3; overlaps as well as

differences between religious and secular are important, 17–18
Fea, John, on whether or not the USA was founded as a Christian nation, 172n3
Firestein, Stuart, 73
Frankl, Victor, 21–22
Freedom, capable of doing evil as well as good, 90; dire ecological consequences of misuses of, 89; human, absence of or escape from as denial of humanity, 90
Future beliefs, unknowability of, 43–46, 53–54

Galileo Galilei, 43, 105
Gericault, Theodore, 113
Ganeles, Diane, 15
God, Jewish conception of as deeply involved in temporal events rather than being timeless, 26–27. *See also* for views of, Bass, Diana Butler; Kauffman, Stuart; Raymo, Chet; Tillich, Paul

Hadith and Sharia, as supplements to the Qur'an, 42
Hägglund, Martin, 17; holds that all religions yearn for a timeless or everlasting afterlife, while secular outlooks affirm both finite life in time and the urgent need for social justice in this life, 18–20, 23, 26–29
Hanh, Thich Nhat, 129
Heaven, belief in not inconsistent with urgency of ecological crisis, 103; necessary presence of ambiguous order in, 85–86; when viewed as timeless, an ominous vision of hell, 22
Heidegger, Martin, 120, 121
Hodge, Alexander, 41

Hogue, Michael, 142
Horseherder, Nicole, 129
Hossenfelder, Sabine, on need for mathematical theories to be empirically confirmed, 171n1
Humility, the virtue of, 144–50
Hypotheses, all claims to truth and value as, and as requiring tests by experience, 72; applies also to religion, 73–78, 80; testing of in Theravada Buddhism, 75–76

James, William, denies possibility of absolute moral values and infallible religious teachings, 45–46
Jesus, 76
Judaism, continuing emphasis on social justice, 28; post-exilic, afterlife (when believed in) as everlasting rather than timeless, and as involving ongoing work, not just rest, 26–28
Judaism, intense prophetic emphasis on social justice in, 26–27; pre-exilic, absence of an afterlife in, 26–27

Kant, Immanuel, his vision of the afterlife as involving everlasting striving and work, 28
Kauffman, Stuart, 10, 104–108, 146, 149; criticism of his identification of creativity of nature with the idea of God, 107–108; focus of the sacred should be on nature, 105; his hope of healing the split between reason and faith, 105; his view compatible with both religious and non-religious views of nature, 106; identifies God with immanent creativity of nature, 104–106; inadequacy of his concept of faith, 106–107; recognition of sacredness of nature does not require

Kauffman, Stuart *(continued)*
  abandoning traditional monotheisms and opting solely for Kauffman's interpretation of this sacredness, 107; a welcome counterforce to ecological irresponsibility, 106
Kierkegaard, Søren, 23
Knowledge, fallibility of all claims to, 4

Laborde, Cécile, 141
Leibniz, Gottfried, 43–44
Locke, John, 12, 139–40

Meland, Bernard Eugene, 57
Morality, a crucial part of but does not require religion, 111; ecological crisis and, 111–12; ethical egoism the antithesis of, 111; Golden Rule and, 111; and the "moral point of view" (Baier), 111; scope of it is universal, including not only humans but all living creatures of earth and their environments, 111–12
Munch, Edvard, 113

Naturajan, Priyamvada, 101, 102
Natural world, flow of time within as a kind of order, 84; human desecrations and mistreatments of, 90; laws of can support or harm, 85; laws of not eternal, 84; would be a chaos without natural laws, 84
Natural world, ambiguities of, 8, 9, 165–67; "blurred ambivalence" of in Daoism, 93; both inevitable and desirable, 98–99; can be religiously affirmed and welcomed, 91; in Daoism and pantheism, 93; despairing, nihilistic response to as a secular phenomenon, 83; in the human side of nature, 89–90; in inanimate nature, 84–86; necessary to any natural order, 85; no escape from in any meaningful concept of heaven, 85–86; in nonhuman animate nature, 86–89; not all religious people seek escape from, 81, 83; no way of avoiding, 88–89; sufferings, dangers, and losses throughout, 87
Naturalism, as a contemporary movement, 96–98; Daoism as example of, 91–93, 96; nature as all there is, but more than enough for religious faith and life, 97–98; nature its own ground in, 96; nothing supernatural in, 96; no personal God in, 96; no personal immortality in, 96; pantheism as example of, 93–96; Raymo as proponent of, 145–46, 160–63; religious, 9, 14–15, 91, 149; sees all claims to truth as probabilistic at best, 97; Spinoza as proponent of, 96; stresses being at home in nature and the responsibility toward nature this entails, 96; unique gifts of humans imply unique responsibilities toward nature on earth, 97; welcomes findings of the natural sciences, 96–97; whole of nature the focus of, 145
Newton, Isaac, 44, 105
Nihilism, as one kind of secularism, 136; as rejection of the sacredness of nature, 107
Nirvana, 23

Oliver, Mary, her view of the sacred, 152, 172n6
Otto, Rudolf, 154

Pantheism, 9, 91, 93–96, 112; an alternative kind of religion, 93;

based fundamentally in feeling, rather than in texts, traditions, or doctrines, 94; no personal God in, 93; no personal immortality in, 94, 95; sacred or divine present in the whole of nature, 94; ultimacy of nature with all its ambiguities in, 93, 94

Peltz, James, 15

Planck, Max, 44

Positivism, Logical, 14

Quenstedt, Johann Andreas, 38

Qur'an, on the sacredness of nature, 107

Raymo, Chet, 135, 145–46, 148, 149, 160–63; as agnostic, atheistic, and pantheistic, 163; contends that all future religions need to be ecumenical, ecological, and embracing of the scientific story of the world, 162–63; does not address ambiguities of the natural world, 165–66; does not endorse an afterlife, 167, 168; emphasizes use of versions of the scientific method in all areas of thought, 160–61 (*see also* in this connection Dewey, John); his use of the metaphor of the great web of nature, 166; insists that science gives us a way to reconceive religion, 161, 168; profoundly open to what can be learned from and affirmed in secular culture, 168–69; rejects anthropomorphic deities and supernatural miracles; calls attention to the miracles of nature instead, 161; sees prayer as reverent attention to the miracles of nature, 161–62; sees the sacred throughout and only within the natural world, 163, 164, 167

Rectification of Names in Confucianism, 119

Reformation, Protestant, lack of consensus about how to interpret and apply biblical teachings in, 39–40

Religions, cannot be replaced by science, 58, 80; cannot substitute for science, 7; claimed to be obsolete, a thing of the past, 58; commonalities with secularism, 137; dangerous character of distinctive cultural role of, 59, 79; difference between sacred and secular turns on focus of the former on the ontological status and import of the sacred, 1, 2, 11; diversity of inevitable and desirable, 50–52, 54; do not all lay claim to infallible or absolute knowledge, 4–6, 58, 79; faith in cannot be forced but can only be persuaded, 139; fallibility of not a defect but an opportunity, 52; as formidable forces for evil as well as good, 172n4; four false views of religion and of religion's differences from secularism, 90–91; fundamental role of existential meaning, purpose, and value in, 73–77; generally deeply concerned with social justice, 3–4; humility a fundamental virtue of, 5; naturalistic kind of, 77–78; increasingly exposed to influence of secular culture, 57; indebtedness to science, 61–66, 79, 145–46; need for convictional openness in, 6; not all world-denying, 9, 10, 58, 81, 83, 85; not fixed or unalterable, 15, 53, 59; not necessarily committed to either timeless or everlasting afterlife, 3, 58, 79; not necessarily opposed to science, 59; not necessarily

Religions *(continued)*
supernatural in focus or appeals to authority, 58–59; not synonymous with faith in God, 156; not synonymous with irrationality, 89; ontology and, 126–31; piety of can be naturalistic, 78; piety of cannot be commanded, 12; possibility of new ones in the future, 44, 53; religious claims to epistemic certainty, 5; right to resist hegemonic science, 60, 74; role in ecological crisis, 10–11; and secular views of reality, 136–37; sense of mystery fundamental to, 6, 77; should use method of science in its reasoning, 8, 60; stereotypical understandings of, 3; turns on an explicit ontology of the sacred, 11, 127–31, 135–36, 142–43; two basic tasks of in relation to secular culture: learning from and being a critic of some aspects of, 6–7; Whitehead's harmony of contrasts idea applicable to, 51

Rest. *See* Work

Rita, 128, 129

Rushdoony, Rousas John, 38–39

Sacred, associations with Buddha-Nature, Brahman-Atman, Daoist Way, God, Goddess, Mandate of Heaven, Navajo religion, Nirvana, Rita, 129–31; cannot dictate to secular culture, 2; central ontological role of in religion, 11, 131, 132, 133, 135–36; common urgent concern of with the secular, 114–15; defining traits of, 11, 18, 127–28; fallibility of, 6; genuine religious sense of, 118; not adamantly opposed to secularism, 137; not something to be trivialized, trifled with, or easily understood, 119; sacred earth, 129, 152. *See also* Bass, Diana Butler; Kauffman, Stuart; Raymo, Chet; Schleiermacher, Friedrich Daniel Ernst; Whitehead, Alfred North

Schaeffer, Francis A., 39; his total opposition to secular humanism, 172n1

Schilbrack, Kevin, 11, 117, 132; functional aspect of religion, 123–24; his analysis of definitions of religion, 122–26; ontological aspect of, 124–25; problems with his analysis of the ontological aspect, 125–26

Schleiermacher, Friedrich Daniel Ernst, 9, 93–96, 112, 146, 149; his concept of the Infinite or what can also be called the sacred, 119

Science, cannot replace religion, 59, 80; decentering effects of earth and humans by, 61–66; impact of on anthropomorphic conceptions of God, 63–64; its method is applicable to religious thought, 80; limitations of, 67–69; natural sciences, 61–64; not a bastion of irrefutable truths, even within its own domain, 69; not entitled to a hegemonic relation to other aspects of culture, including religion, 59–60, 66, 71, 79; only one dimension of culture, 79; particular fields of different from basic method of, 7–8, 60, 69–78, 79; possibility of a new scientific revolution in the future, 43; restricted scope of, 59; social sciences, 64–66, 69; strictly objective method of cannot substitute for the human need for firsthand, existential

meaning, purpose, and value, 67, 68, 73–77; typically descriptive and explanatory, not in the business of assessing or justifying basic value commitments, 68; values implicit in and presupposed by the enterprise of science, 68–69, 70–71
Scientism. *See* Secularism, scientific version of
Scriptures, religious, as dictated by God, 38; claimed inerrancy of not tenable, 37–42, 45; two problems with claimed inerrancy of, 39
Scruton, Roger, 131
Secularism, cannot be distinguished from all religions on the claimed ground of the latters' insistence on the absolute truth of its claims, rejection of the ambiguities of nature, centering on a personal deity or deities, opposing the sciences, being committed to supernaturalism, or being committed a timeless or everlasting afterlife, 4–6, 55, 117–18; does not focus on the distinctively religious meaning, ontology, or role of the sacred, 119–20, 130, 135–36; earlier meanings of, 12, 137–38; and nihilism, 136; ontological commitments of not always clear, 136; and religious views of reality, 136–37; scientific version of, 70; secular uses of the term *sacred*, 108–109; should not try to substitute for the sacred, 2; value, importance, and essential role of, 130. *See also* Religions; Schilbrack, Kevin; Tillich, Paul
Secular state, allows for commonalities of civil commitment, 140; allows for religious and secular diversity and freedom, 12, 140; concept of, 138–42; danger of intermingling of certain earlier religious ideas with present secular ones in, 141–42; John Locke's view of, 139–40; on religious neutrality of, 139–40; respectful of religion, not opposed to it, 139
Shakespeare, William, 113
Spinoza, Baruch, 96, 105

Tauber, Alfred I., 70–71
Taylor, Barbara Brown, 76
Taylor, Charles, 143
Thirty Years' War, 5, 40
Tillich, Paul, 13, 131–32; concept of a personal God symbolical not literal, 121; on the power of Being-itself, 120–21; his view of the nature of religion too broad and is prescriptive rather than descriptive, 118, 121; mistaken in thinking that all ultimate concerns are those of religious faith, 142; on the narrower and larger concepts of religion, 120–22; recognition of need for an ontological focus in concepts of religion a virtue of his view, 12; religion distinct from secularism only in the narrow sense of religion, 121
Time, absence of unimaginable and unrealizable, 25; combines continuity and novelty, 24; contingencies and uncertainties of life in, 5; life in something to be grateful for and fervently affirmed rather than begrudged, 31–32; no biological evolution without, 24–25; ordinary matter as outcome of, 25; presupposed by change, 24; as primordial and universal, 23–25; saturates human experience, 24; timeless life a contradiction, 24

Timeless life, illusion of, 23–26; not the goal of all religions, 22–23; stout religious faith fully consistent with the finality of death, 32–33; tedium, pointlessness, and undesirability of, 20–23
Tradition, religious, as necessary supplement to scriptures, 40
Truth, absolute, not attainable for four reasons, 36–37; claim to not a defining trait of all religion, 35–36, 51; example of controversy over in contemporary approaches to same-sex marriage and ordination in the United Methodist Church, 48–50; fallibility of all claims to, 37–43, 72–73; great dangers in claims to clearly shown in history, 46–50; such fallibility does not imply epistemological relativism and can motivate continuing searches for deeper, more comprehensive understanding in religion and all other fields of experience and thought, 52; two descriptive and two prescriptive obstacles to assertions of, 52–54
Truths, tests of. *See* Hypotheses

Ultimate concern nor restricted to religion, 12–13. *See also* Tillich, Paul
Ultimates, religious, indescribable mystery of, 37

Values, tests of. *See* Hypotheses
Venn Diagram view of relations of sacred and secular, 151
Vienna Circle, 147–49; no cognitive meaning or truth value for religion in, 148; no room for mystery in, 148; at opposite extreme of intolerance from ultraconservative Christians, 147, 148–49; relentless scientism of, 147, 148

Waley, Arthur, 92
Warfield, Benjamin, 41
Whitehead, Alfred North, 51, 73–74; his concept of permanent rightness equivalent to the sacred, 128
Wilson, E. O., 10, 108; but it also points the way to a much needed confluence of the sacred and the secular in relation to the ecological crisis, 108; his approach is also secular, not religious, 108; his approach to the crisis eminently practical but also moral, 108
Wohlleben, Peter, 86
Work correlative with rest, 26
Wu, Kuang-ming, 92

www.ingramcontent.com/pod-product-compliance
Lightning Source LLC
Chambersburg PA
CBHW021142230426
43667CB00005B/227